Practical Skills for Police Community Support Officers

Practical Skills for Police Community Support Officers

Sue Madsen

LawMatters
PUBLISHING

Published by Law Matters Publishing
Law Matters Limited
33 Southernhay East
Exeter EX1 1NX
Tel: 01392 215577

British Library Cataloguing-in-Publication Data

A catalogue record for this book is available from the British Library.

ISBN: 978 1 84641 040 6

Typeset by Pantek Arts Ltd, Maidstone, Kent

Printed by Cromwell Press Ltd, Trowbridge, Wiltshire

Contents

Introduction

The introduction of a clearly defined Police Community Support Officer (PCSO) role into the modern police service will dramatically increase the presence of the police on the streets. It will also help provide reassurance to the public and enhance community policing. A PCSO is therefore an integral part of the police service and the efforts of the police to deliver the best possible service to communities. The role of PCSO does not exist to create different levels of policing. It is a new and unique role which will create a wider policing team and help deliver greater public reassurance and deal with quality-of-life issues.

This book allows PCSOs to transfer the knowledge and skills obtained during their initial training into the workplace using practical policing scenarios. The book will be a useful manual for the newly appointed PCSO as well as a helpful guidance document for those already in post. Those wishing to apply for the role of PCSO may also find the book useful as preparation for the assessment process.

Structure of the book

Chapter 1

Outlines the PCSO role profile, competencies and police powers.

Chapter 2

Provides an explanation of the skills and abilities required of a PCSO. This includes coverage of the National Occupational Standards (NOS) allocated to the role and how they will be used in workplace assessment.

Chapters 3–9

Each of these chapters examines a potential policing issue using scenario-based examples. The scenarios have been chosen to reflect the type of problems PCSOs regularly encounter. The issues covered are as follows:

- *Effective foot patrol* – preparing and conducting effective foot patrol, following up intelligence and information, dealing with property and keeping a beat profile.

- *Anti-social behaviour* – the current problem of youth nuisance and disorder, the effect that it can have on communities and how to implement a Problem-Oriented Policing (POP) plan.

- *Community meetings* – preparing, attending and documenting community meetings.

- *Licensing* – alcohol misuse and the corresponding licensing issues.

- *Traffic-related duties* – commonplace minor traffic-related issues such as obstruction and parking.

- *Motor vehicle nuisance* – anti-social use of motor vehicles including off-road motorcycles, issue of warning notices and seizure of vehicles.

- *Statement writing* – how to formulate and complete a range of witness statements.

How to make the most of the scenarios

Each chapter provides an introduction to the scenario and places it within the context of the police service. All of the scenarios in this book reflect actual incidents and details of the incident are carefully outlined to provide you with all the information you need to progress methodically through the scenario. The scenarios are also broken down into the following five key areas to encourage a logical thought process:

- *Identify the problem*

- *Research the problem*

- *Develop a plan*

- *Implement the plan*

- *Action to be taken*

At times other headings will be used to encourage the reader to look further into the scenario. However, overall the structure will remain the same.

In a similar way to an actual incident, the scenario may change and new dilemmas may be encountered that require you to make a decision. The chapters therefore reflect the changing environment PCSOs work within. Throughout the scenarios you are asked a series of pertinent questions which are answered outlining the actions you might consider taking. These questions are repeated at regular junctures during the scenario to help you develop structured problem-solving techniques. The questions used are:

- *What do you know?*

- *What do you need to know?*

- *How are you going to find that out?*

- *What next?*

This process can be transferred into the workplace and will provide a good basis for dealing with issues when performing the role of PCSO on a day-to-day basis.

At the end of each scenario a flowchart has been included to provide an at-a-glance guide to dealing with the given scenarios. The flowchart follows the same structure as the scenario and gives bullet point advice regarding options or avenues that can be taken by the PCSO attending or dealing with the specific issue.

Methods of assessment

At the beginning of each of the scenario-based chapters you will find a list of the National Occupational Standards (NOS) relevant to the scenario. During the chapter you will also notice shaded boxes indicating which of the NOS for PCSOs are achieved by the completion of individual sections of the scenario. These will help you identify the information you need to submit when undertaking workplace assessment to meet the required competencies for the role of PCSO.

PCSOs are often required to maintain a portfolio to record their achievements, workplace performance and any additional training. These portfolios are often referred to as the 'Personal Development Portfolio' or 'Professional Development Portfolio', but the name can differ between forces. This book highlights opportunities for portfolio development using the following symbol:

Portfolio symbol: 🗁

The PCSO role profile is comprised of three key elements: core responsibilities, activities and behaviours. The role profile and its structure will be examined in more detail in Chapter 1 of this book; however, it is worth noting here that PCSOs are continually assessed against the activities and behaviours inherent in their role profile. The assessment of a PCSO's role behaviours/activities can take a number of different forms depending on the police force they work within. Assessment is regularly undertaken through performance development reviews or as part of their development portfolio (again, this may differ between forces). Opportunities for the reader to reflect on the role profile activities and behaviours are indicted in the shaded boxes in the scenarios by the following symbol:

Role profile activities/Behaviour symbol: ❖

The reader should also be aware that at the time of going to print a new PCSO National Vocational Qualification (NVQ) is currently being developed. The introduction of this qualification could mean a PCSO is required to complete an NVQ, if directed by their individual force. If an NVQ does come into effect, a PCSO could use the NOS highlighted throughout this book to help them meet and understand the necessary role profile criteria. The methods of assessment for an NVQ may differ from those mentioned in this book. It is therefore important the reader agrees with their assessor how evidence of their performance against the NOS needs to be produced to complete the NVQ.

Chapter 1

Role of the Police Community Support Officer

Introduction

In order to gain the maximum benefit from this book it is important the reader first and foremost understands what the role profile and job requirements of the Police Community Support Officer (PCSO) are. This chapter will explain the PCSO role profile in simple terms, outlining the powers and job requirements granted to PCSOs within the police force. You will also gain a greater understanding of how changes to the police service as a whole, such as government initiatives, training schemes and assessment methods, will help integrate the PCSO into the policing family.

This chapter may also be useful to those hoping to apply to become a PCSO as the current application and assessment processes are based upon the role profile/competencies explained during this chapter.

The role

The PCSO role is a unique and valuable one to the police service if it is performed well.

The government has recently implemented a Neighbourhood Policing Policy to be adopted by all forces; this policy describes the PSCO as the eyes and ears of the service with a responsibility to address the spectrum of anti-social behaviour issues. Over the past few years, due to the growing demands on the police service, the area of community policing has changed. Resources have not been available to maintain certain functions such as high visibility patrols etc. This, among other factors, has increased a fear of crime in the community. By broadening the policing family with the introduction of the PCSO, forces can support front-line policing by allocating relevant tasks to PCSOs, such as high-visibility patrols. This will enable police officers to deal with the more complex and high-risk tasks that require their extended powers.

National Occupational Standards

The National Occupational Standards (NOS) form the basis of the PCSO job description. The PCSO role profile, training and assessment are all developed from these standards. The NOS for the role of PCSO are monitored and updated by an organisation named Skills for Justice (the dedicated Sector Skills Council and Standards Body for the Justice Sector). They work alongside justice sector organisations and identify the skills, priorities and actions required for workplace development.

Many of the NOS for a PCSO are the same as those for a student police officer. Some standards, however, have been specifically created for the role of PCSO. We will continue to explore the NOS in more detail in Chapter 2.

PCSO powers

At present, the powers granted a PCSO are selected by the Chief Officer in each individual force. This means there is no common ground, or standardisation of powers, allocated to PCSOs across the country. PCSOs in different forces will have different powers to deal with incidents. The government plans to address this lack of standardisation and are considering a set of national powers for all PCSOs. A proposal regarding the standardisation of PCSO powers was introduced to Parliament via the Police and Justice Bill in January 2006, but this proposal needs to complete the parliamentary process before it becomes statutory.

There are, however, clear guidelines from the Association of Chief Police Officers (ACPO) on incidents when PCSOs should *not* be used. These are:

- where there is a clear likelihood that confrontation will arise;
- where there is scope to use a high degree of discretion;
- where any action taken by police is likely to lead to a higher than normal risk of harm to any person;
- where there is a clear likelihood that any police action taken will be an infringement of human rights;
- where the incident could lead to a significant amount of further work.

Standardised powers

Skills for Justice have produced a suggested list of standardised powers for a PCSO. In descriptions of the PCSO role profile, NOS or practical scenarios, this book concentrates on the powers outlined by Skills for Justice (See Appendix A).

Role profile

Within the police service a competency framework known as the **Integrated Competency Framework (ICF)** has been introduced. This framework outlines the required competencies for the individual roles within the police service. The introduction of the ICF has ensured a common standard for individual role profiles throughout the service. The ICF can be used to plan training needs, compile job descriptions, assist recruitment and monitor staff to improve performance.

A role profile will form the basis of any performance review or appraisal carried out on a role holder. The competencies relevant to the role profile ensure the person or task is assessed against a set of agreed standards. Role competencies therefore help to enforce a structured, transparent and objective assessment process which can be used by supervisors, managers or the post holders themselves to gather evidence of performance. A role profile will also state the relevant National Occupational Standards upon which the profile has been formulated.

Role profiles may differ slightly between forces simply because the job requirements vary in each policing area. PCSOs are no exception to this and their role profile will often be specific to a particular force and/or policing requirements. Nevertheless the core elements of the PCSO role profile (generic skills) are the same across the police service.

Skills for Justice have produced a role profile for the PCSO and this will be used as a benchmark for this book (see Appendix B). Any additional role profile information you require can be requested from your local police force and dealt with using the same principles you will see outlined within the book.

Structure of a role profile

A role profile is made up of core responsibilities, activities and behaviours. We will explore each in turn:

- *Core Responsibilities*. As the title suggests, these are the areas of responsibility that are central to the role profile; examples of these for the PCSO role are Community Safety and Intelligence.

- *Activities*. These are the specific tasks/activities that a person is expected to perform in their role. Activities are explained in a role profile and grouped together under the relevant core responsibility area. Each activity is allocated an activity number.

- *Behaviours*. The areas/standards of behaviour expected of a person carrying out a role are separated into behaviour areas and behaviour descriptions. Behaviours are not to be dealt with in isolation as the standard of behaviour can easily affect the activities. To achieve competence in a role three different levels of behaviour need to be attained, usually at levels A, B or C (Respect for Race and Diversity behaviour is always a level A). Examples of behaviours for the role of PCSO are Working with Others and Achieving Results.

Throughout the practical scenario chapters of this book you will be reminded of the appropriate PCSO role behaviours/activities in one of two ways. First of all, at the very beginning of each chapter you will find a table listing the National Occupational Standards and the activities/behaviours relevant to the scenario as a whole. Secondly, at regular points during the scenario there are a series of shaded boxes which remind you of the PCSO activities/behaviours appropriate to particular sections of the scenario. The activities/behaviours will be indicated in the shaded boxes by the following symbol: ❖

See Appendix B for a detailed example of a role profile.

Chapter 2
Skills and abilities

Introduction

In the previous chapter we explored the Integrated Competency Framework (ICF) and the contents of a role profile for a PCSO. In this chapter we will examine the specific skills and abilities required to competently perform the role of PCSO. We will consider how the NOS underpin the skills, abilities, training and development of PCSOs. We will also look at how the PCSO may be continually monitored and assessed against the NOS within the workplace.

Training and development

It has been recommended the training and development of newly appointed PCSOs follows the same structure as that of Student Police Officers. A national recruitment process has been implemented for the role of PCSO which is very similar to the process Police Officer recruits undergo. The PCSO recruitment process involves a role-related Assessment Centre which concentrates on the competencies (NOS) required of a person to fulfil the role of PCSO.

The government has recently introduced the Wider Policing Learning and Development Programme which encourages integration of the training and development of PCSOs with other groups of the police service. All PCSO training is mapped against the NOS to ensure its relevance to the role and the preparation of the individual for the workplace. Other methods of training and assessment for both Police Officers and PCSO recruits generally take the form of a workplace achievement portfolio.

Work-based assessment

Assessing competence in a job using the NOS has been used by many different sectors in the past. Work-based assessment is now commonly used within the police service in a variety of areas, including criminal investigation training, the Initial Police Learning and Development Programme (IPLDP) and Sergeant/ Inspector promotion processes. The PCSO is no exception to this and the role holder will be assessed within the workplace.

National Occupational Standards

National Occupational Standards (NOS) outline the key competencies and knowledge necessary for certain job roles. When coupled with an assessment strategy, they provide clear guidelines for the assessment of competence in a specific job role against nationally agreed standards of performance. NOS are widely used to provide benchmarks of best practice across the United Kingdom. They can also form a qualification for the relevant role holder, including a National Vocational Qualification (NVQ). The NOS are particularly important to the police service as they offer a set of competency guidelines which are flexible enough to meet the specific needs of different forces. For the role of PCSO this flexibility is particularly useful as the powers allocated and role profiles given to PCSOs will differ between constabularies.

Structure of National Occupational Standards

The NOS are grouped together by Skills for Justice into particular occupational areas/sectors. For PCSOs the NOS are taken from the policing and law enforcement sector. The NOS are broken down into individual **units**. These units describe competent performance and are made up of a number of individual parts which combine to fulfil the required outcomes and role competencies.

- **Unit summary**. This describes what the unit is about and how it fits into the workplace. It may outline the type of incidents or activities to which the unit applies. Each unit is given a number, for example 1A1.

- **Elements**. Units are divided into elements. A unit can be comprised of anything between one and five individual elements. An element consists of **performance criteria** and **range**.

- **Performance criteria**. The element will contain a list of performance criteria. These clearly describe the performance required by the role holder to achieve competence. (They should not be treated as a list of tasks.)

- **Range**. Within the performance criteria certain areas are highlighted to suggest a range of possible applications. When a range is given this means candidates will need to demonstrate competence within the performance criteria and across the specified range.

- **Knowledge and understanding**. This is what a role holder will need to know and understand in order to perform competently within the unit. This is the basic underpinning knowledge and understanding of policies, procedures, facts, opinions, theories, etc. This is the final part of a unit and will cover the whole unit.

- *Evidence requirements*. These outline the evidence required by the role holder in order to achieve competency in the unit. They may state, for example, that the performance criteria need to be displayed on a given number of separate occasions or that the range is required a specific number of times.

National Occupational Standards for Police Community Support Officers

Although the NOS are agreed by individual forces according to the particular role-profile activities they have created, this book utilises the generic PCSO role profile. An NVQ qualification for PCSOs is currently being developed and, as mentioned in the previous chapter, standardised powers for the role are also being considered. Until these have been approved and in use, it will be up to the individual force to decide how many NOS will be assessed. If the units are assessed and accredited as part of a recognised qualification such as an NVQ, the PCSO can carry their accredited units over should they decide to pursue a career as a Police Officer, for example. Carrying over previously attained units in this way is called the accreditation of prior learning (APL). APL is dependent on an individual's circumstances and will need to be clarified with the relevant awarding body for the qualification.

The following list outlines the standards most easily achievable within the role of PCSO. Some of the units are applicable to Police Officers while other units have been specifically created for PCSOs. Where a unit is for a PCSO this is indicated in brackets as 'PCSO only' next to the unit heading:

1A1 – Use police actions in a fair and justified way

This focuses on the use of officer actions and applies across the use of all police powers. Police actions must be used proportionately and fairly and be legitimate, necessary and lawful within the circumstances.

- This could include stop/search/detention/issue of tickets or in fact any action taken by an officer.

1A4 – Foster people's equality, diversity and rights

The acknowledgement of equality and diversity, including a person's rights and responsibilities, is the principal aim of this particular occupational standard. It also includes the need for confidentiality, particularly when handling sensitive information. It is expected the PCSO will be proactive against discrimination and will try to diffuse any specific tensions arising in an individual or among different people. The term 'people' includes individuals, families, groups, communities and organisations, or anyone else you may come into contact with.

- This could include any situations dealt with that may include an element of the following: race/ethnicity, religion/faith, sexual orientation, social status, poverty, physical/learning disability, mental health, age, gender/sex, migrants, asylum seekers, travellers, non-English-speaking groups, single parents, unemployed, students, mixed heritage, family status, political belief, etc.

(This list is not exhaustive but gives an idea of the scope of this unit which can usually be evidenced within all areas of day-to-day duties.)

1B9 – Provide initial support to individuals affected by offending or anti-social behaviour and assess their needs for further support

This looks at the initial contact and further support a PCSO might give to individuals who have been affected by offending or anti-social behaviour. Further support can be dependent on the needs and wishes of the individual and can be practical or emotional. This could simply involve listening to and reassuring the individual or arranging other support over a period of time. This may include court cases, those severely affected by their experience or those that are vulnerable. The individual may need to be assessed and any further support that they, or their family may need, agreed and discussed, taking into account the wishes of the individual and the available resources. Sometimes you may need to balance the rights of the individual with any possible risks of harm to them or to others. It may also be necessary to seek advice and support from colleagues or specialists, especially if the individual is a child, in which instance parental responsibility should be sought. The term 'individual' can refer to the person to whom you are providing support, a victim/survivor of offending or anti-social behaviour, or the family and friends of a victim, especially in the case of bereaved families.

- This could include any situations dealt with that involve victims/witnesses or others involved that are affected by offending or anti-social behaviour. This could range from minor crime/disorder to more serious offences or road traffic incidents/collisions.

1B11 – Contribute to resolving community issues (PCSO only)

This is about helping to resolve community issues and may involve quality of life, tensions, minor disorder or anti-social behaviour. They may be of a large or small geographical area. It involves developing and maintaining good communication links with communities and respecting the culture, religion and race/ethnicity of others. Communities are neighbourhoods, communities of interest (e.g. businesses), communities of identity (e.g. older people, minority ethnic groups, young people, lesbians, gay men, asylum seekers and travellers).

- To resolve community issues will involve firstly identifying them, then using problem-solving approaches, working in partnership with other agencies and taking the appropriate action, while also supporting those affected by the issues.

2A1 – Gather and submit information that has the potential to support policing objectives

This is about gathering information that has the potential to become intelligence and is therefore likely to assist with and support policing objectives. This unit works in accordance with the National Intelligence Model (NIM).

- To achieve this information must be identified from a variety of situations and sources (human and technical) that has the potential to become intelligence. The role holder will need to conduct an initial assessment and grading of that information. The correct submission of intelligence reports from a variety of different sources in relation to different areas/incidents will help towards becoming competent in this unit.

2C4 – Minimise and deal with aggressive and abusive behaviour

This unit is about acting in a way that does not provoke aggressive or abusive behaviour. It also covers defusing situations and protecting yourself when dealing with people who are, or may become, aggressive and abusive by breaking away from the situation. *There is no requirement in this unit to use physical force.*

- This can be evidenced when in this type of situation by:
  - showing respect for people, their property and their rights;
  - identifying and minimising any actions or words that may trigger abusive/aggressive behaviour;
  - taking constructive action to defuse situations;
  - acting in a way that is calm and reassuring;
  - physically breaking away, if necessary, from a threatening situation in a safe and effective manner.

2C5 – Contribute to providing an initial response to incidents (PCSO only)

This is about contributing to providing an initial response to incidents that may be encountered during duties. These may include critical incidents, public order, crime allegations or non-crime incidents, racist incidents or other hate crime, youth nuisance and anti-social behaviour.

- Gathering information on the incidents can evidence this, e.g. history, dangers, witness details, etc., then using that information gathered to establish the nature of the incident and plan your actions accordingly. This process may happen quickly on route to an incident or while dealing with it at the time. Health and safety needs to be considered when responding to incidents.

2J3 – Present information to courts or other hearings (PCSO only)

This unit is about preparing and presenting information to courts and other hearings.

- This can be evidenced by correctly dealing with a criminal court warning or requests from other hearings such as a coroner's court, criminal injury compensation agencies or a civil court, then presenting information in an effective manner complying with the rules and procedures required.

4G2 – Ensure your own actions reduce risks to health and safety

This unit is about having an appreciation of significant risks in the workplace and knowing how to identify and deal with them. To gain competency a person must ensure that their own actions do not create any risks, that they do not ignore significant risks within the workplace and that they take sensible action to put things right, e.g. reporting situations that could pose a risk, or danger, or seeking advice from the appropriate person.

- Reporting incidents to the responsible person, taking action to avoid/minimise risks or hazards and carrying out tasks safely in accordance with instructions and workplace requirements can evidence this. This evidence is likely to occur within day-to-day duties.

4G4 – Administer First Aid

This is about the application of First Aid in emergency situations. It covers the ability to respond promptly and appropriately to a range of situations and incidents in order to preserve life and protect casualties until specialist aid is available.

- This can be evidenced by completion of a recognised First Aid Award or by actual First Aid applied in day-to-day situations. Due to the nature of the role of a police officer or PCSO it is unlikely that all of the evidence will be achieved using real situations, therefore simulations or role plays may be used. These are normally incorporated into training for a recognised award.

1E5 – Contribute to road safety (PCSO only)

This focuses on road safety and the PCSO does not need to have specific traffic warden powers in order to achieve this unit. It covers the ability to identify and deal with incidents, respond to hazards appropriately and use safety equipment when required. The role holder must be able to take account of prevailing conditions (e.g. weather, road type), pass on information to other agencies (e.g. emergency services, highway authorities) and complete any necessary documentation.

- This can be evidenced by responding to ongoing incidents/collisions, placing, moving or removing cones or signs, directing traffic and setting up road blocks for events or occasions.

2C6 – Contribute to planned policing operations (PCSO only)

This unit is about contributing to planned policing operations and applies to all types of pre-planned operations, e.g. crowd control, football matches, demonstrations, marches, galas and the use of automatic number plate recorders (ANPRs).

- The post holder will need to prepare themselves for the operation, be clear about their role and responsibilities, obtain the right equipment and complete the relevant documentation. They will also need to actually participate in the operation, carry out their role and responsibilities as per the briefing, use the authorised equipment correctly and co-ordinate their actions with others involved in the operation.

2I1 – Search individuals

This unit is about searching individuals for items suspected as being evidence of an offence or for the prevention of harm to self or others. The officer must first ensure that they have the grounds and legal authority to carry out the search (PCSOs must have been allocated this power by the chief officer in order to achieve this unit).

- This can be achieved by identifying and dealing with any potential risks present (e.g. weapons, risk of violence being used, sharps, hazardous substances or warning signs). The search must be conducted in a legal, ethical manner using approved techniques. Any evidence found is to be seized, packaged and stored correctly maintaining integrity and continuity. The search results need to be communicated to the individual and other relevant persons and any document required must be completed in the correct manner.

Throughout the practical scenario chapters of this book links will be made to the areas where, during the day-to-day duties of a PCSO the NOS can be achieved and used as evidence of performance in a portfolio.

These will be indicated by the portfolio symbol: 🗁

To assist in the navigation of the book in relation to the NOS the following matrix will show at a glance the NOS that are covered in each chapter:

NOS	Chapters						
	3	4	5	6	7	8	9
1A1		•		•	•	•	
1A4	•	•	•	•	•	•	•
1B9	•	•					
1B11	•	•	•	•	•	•	
1E5					•	•	
2A1	•	•	•	•		•	
2C4		•					
2C5	•	•		•	•	•	
2C6		•		•	•		
2J3							•
4G2	•			•	•	•	

Chapter 3
Effective foot patrol

This chapter covers criteria within the following units of the **National Occupational Standards** for Police Community Support Officers:

1A4   Foster people's equality, diversity and rights

1B9   Provide initial support to individuals affected by offending or anti-social behaviour and assess their needs for further support

1B11 Contribute to resolving community issues (PCSO)

2A1   Gather and submit information that has the potential to support policing objectives

2C5   Contribute to providing an initial response to incidents (PCSO)

4G2   Ensure your own actions reduce the risks to health and safety.

It is likely that the following **activities and behaviours** from the PCSO role profile will also be evidenced:

Activities:

131 – Adopt a problem-solving approach to community issues

112 – Conduct patrol

  1 – Conduct initial investigation

 33 – Manage scene preservation

 74 – Provide care for victims and witnesses

 57 – Use intelligence to support policing objectives

101 – Provide an initial response to incidents

206 – Comply with health and safety legislation

216 – Complete administration procedures

242 – Make best use of technology

141 – Promote equality, diversity and human rights in working practices

127 – Provide an organisation response recognising the needs of all communities

224 – Work as part of a team

Behaviours:

- **Respect for race and diversity**
- **Team working**
- **Community and customer focus**
- **Effective communication**
- **Personal responsibility**
- **Resilience**

Introduction

The National Reassurance Policing Programme involves communities identifying and prioritising local crime and disorder issues, which they tackle together with the police and other public services. Sometimes certain crimes and disorders can have a disproportionate impact on public feelings of safety. The police conducting high-visibility, effective foot patrols within a community is proven to encourage genuine community engagement. This has led to local people taking ownership of their neighbourhoods in partnership with the police and other agencies. Almost all forces view 'fear of crime' as a priority to address and conducting effective foot patrols should lead to communities that feel and are much safer.

The scenario

You have received a written request from the Community Sergeant to provide foot patrol to the Kingston Park area in order to show a police presence and provide the local community with some reassurance. Following the last parish meeting the clerk has raised some concerns about policing in the area. The Sergeant would like this issue addressed prior to the next meeting which is due to be held in one month's time.

IDENTIFY THE PROBLEM

What do you know?

The Sergeant has spoken to the Kingston Park parish council clerk who has concerns regarding an issue in the area. You have been directed to carry out foot patrols in the area to provide police presence and public reassurance.

What do you need to know?
- What are the parish council's specific concerns?

- Who, if anyone, is affected? How can they be contacted?

- Are there any specific days/times to provide the patrols?

How are you going to find that out?
- Contact the Community Sergeant for further information.

What next?
- Acknowledge receipt of the information and accept responsibility for the issue.

- Familiarise yourself with the Kingston Park area.

You contact the Sergeant and confirm that you received the request and that you will be dealing with this. At this point you ask the Sergeant for the further details that you require.

The Sergeant tells you that recently there has been a spate of shed burglaries in the area where lawnmowers and gardening equipment have been stolen. Full details of these are on the communications incident systems and they have been recorded as crimes. The local residents are now worried and feel that the police are not interested in their problem.

The clerk of the parish council has full details of the residents that have raised concerns and they are more than happy to speak to an officer.

RESEARCH THE PROBLEM

What do you know?
That there has been a spate of shed burglaries. This has worried the residents who appear to have a lack of confidence in the police response. The parish council clerk has the details of the people who have raised concerns.

What do you need to know?
- Details of the residents.

- If there are any other current policing issues in the area.

- When and where the crimes have taken place.

- What police action has been taken to date.

How are you going to find that out?
- Contact the parish clerk and obtain details of the residents.

- Check the computer intelligence systems and speak to other local officers regarding any current policing issues in the area.

- Interrogate communications and/or crime recording systems to find details of the crimes that have occurred.

- Contact the attending/Investigating Officers of the crimes to ascertain the status of the investigations.

What next?

You ascertain that six overnight burglaries have taken place in the last two weeks. All of them occurred between 8 p.m. and 8 a.m., within a three-mile radius, in the Kingston Park area.

The Investigating Officer informs you that there is a suspect for these crimes. The investigation is still ongoing and they will inform you of any progress as and when it occurs as they are not in a position to arrest the suspect yet.

The residents tell you that they are very concerned that they are in the middle of a crime wave and this is the start of the area going downhill. They state the situation is affecting their quality of life, as they are now in constant fear of their property or themselves being attacked. They feel they rarely see the police unless something happens and that the police are not interested in the area as normally very little crime occurs. They feel that they do not get a suitable amount of police attention and they are unhappy with this level of service.

What do you know?

- The amount of crimes, dates, times and the area in which they occurred.

- There is a suspect for the offences and the investigations are still ongoing.

- The residents are unhappy with the police attention given to the area.

What do you need to know?

- How to plan your patrols to get the best results for the residents.

How are you going to find that out?

- Speak to experienced Beat Officers/PCSOs/supervision.

What next?

You have a meeting with the Beat Officer covering the area and they ask you to consider the following points when planning your patrols:

1. Ensure that you have all of the information you require for your patrols – e.g. current intelligence, recent crimes or incidents that have occurred.

2. Clarify any information that is not clear, or you do not understand.

3. Know who the key community figures are and where they reside – examples could be parish or local councillors, group leaders of youth groups or other community groups, for example.

4. Be aware of any schools within the area and introduce yourself to the teachers and pupils.

5. Identify any shops in the area and make sure that you visit and introduce yourself.

6. Check if there are any licensed premises within the area. If there are, check the licensing files for information regarding any incidents recorded at them. Introduce yourself to the licensee.

7. Identify any areas that may be vulnerable to crime or nuisance behaviour.

8. Know the layout of the area, where the main roads are, shortcuts to take, parks or recreational areas, etc.

9. Ensure that a beat profile is developed and maintained for the area. (A beat profile is simply a record of any actions/initiatives that have been taken by police in the area. It may also include details of visits or patrols that have taken place and any incidents that have been highlighted. This allows local officers/supervision to look at a profile and have some idea of what has recently been done in terms of policing in a specific area.)

Planning your beat

You now proceed to plan how you will effectively patrol your beat.

- You have already obtained all of the information you require in relation to current intelligence, crimes and incidents within the area.

- You have decided to conduct foot patrol wearing high-visibility police clothing during daylight hours. You will park the police vehicle you use on the main street outside the newsagent store to be fully visible and encourage interaction with people.

- The foot areas that you will cover concentrate in particular on the specific three-mile radius of crime, but will also encompass a similar residential area located in Kingston Park.

- You will also patrol the front street area, outside the school area at school finishing time and the area around the shops. These are prime areas for you to meet local residents and interact with them. This has a dual purpose, as residents will not only see you in the area, but this will provide reassurance that the police are patrolling. It will also enable you to introduce yourself, obtain any information that anyone may wish to give and allow you to give out your contact details for future assistance.

- Part of your plan is to visit each victim, ascertain any further information and provide reassurance that police action is being taken.

- You have based your plan on information from within and outside the police service and recorded it in a beat profile. This will prove a valuable document to record your actions for the information of others as well as yourself. It will also act as a reference document for use in the future to assist with any similar issues.

DEVELOP A PLAN

What do you know?
- That you have now planned your foot patrol and you are ready to carry this out.

What do you need to know?
- What equipment you will need to have with you.

How are you going to find that out?
- Refer back to your initial training.

- Ask colleagues/supervision.

What next?
You refer back to your training and decide that you require the following equipment in order to be safe and effective during your foot patrol:

- personal radio;

- uniform – including any protective items issued (vest, footwear, etc.);

- any relevant forms/paperwork that you may be required to complete (pocket notebook, receipt book, etc.).

You also conduct the following prior to commencing patrol in order to ensure your health and safety:

- Personal radio to be checked as in good working order prior to patrol, with sufficient battery power to last the patrol.

- Communications to be informed of your location and duties so that communication with colleagues can be maintained.

- All uniform and protective items to be checked to ensure that they are fit for purpose and in good working order.

- Ensure that you are fully aware of the correct procedures for use of all equipment.

❖ 57, 242, 141, 224, 206

🗁 2A1, 1B11, 1A4, 4G2

IMPLEMENT THE PLAN

The following day you are on duty 08.00–16.00; you are due to commence foot patrol in the Kingston Park area at 08.30 a.m.

You commence foot patrol as per your plan and are visiting Mr and Mrs May, the victims of one of the recent shed burglaries. Mr May tells you that prior to being broken into, they honestly believed that the small padlock used to secure the shed door was sufficient security to protect their belongings. They stated that they had never given this a second thought and had received no advice to the contrary until the burglary had happened.

Mr and Mrs May feel that when the police attended the burglary and gave them the relevant advice about the lack of security and the poor lock this was helpful, but too late and a case of shutting the stable door after the horse has bolted.

What do you know?

Prior to the burglaries the area appears to have had no crime prevention advice regarding security. As a result this has reinforced the feeling that the police are not interested in the problem or the area.

What do you need to know?

- Have any crime advice/prevention measures been arranged for the area?

- What is the situation with other residents?

- Would the residents welcome crime prevention advice?

How are you going to find that out?

- Contact other residents and check their opinion and the type of security that they already have in place.

- Liaise with Crime Prevention/Community Safety Department and ascertain if/when any input or attention was last given to the area.

What next?

You have visited the other victims of the recent crimes and spoken to other residents. They all have insufficient security measures in place and were keen to receive advice to help improve security as soon as possible.

The Crime Prevention/Community Safety Department has checked records and the area is not specifically identified for attention as yet. The last time a campaign was conducted in that area was three years ago.

You decide to hold a meeting with Crime Prevention/Community Safety Department who suggest a leaflet is circulated to residents outlining the necessary security measures and contact numbers for further advice. They are unable to arrange this, but can assist with ordering the leaflets on your behalf.

You believe that this will assist in reducing the fear of crime and also build relationships between the police and residents. At this stage you liaise with the Community Sergeant who believes this is a good idea and authorises you to go ahead with this project, but is unable to provide any funding for the leaflets.

ACTION TO BE TAKEN

What do you know?

- That there is a need for crime prevention advice to be given in the area.

- That the police are able to obtain the relevant leaflets but cannot provide the funding or resources to distribute them.

What do you need to know?
- Who can provide the funding and how?

How are you going to find that out?
- Speak to colleagues/supervision for advice.

What next?
The Sergeant advises you to contact the Community Safety Partnership representative from the council to request funding for this project. You do this and submit a written request for consideration at the next partnership meeting. The representative contacts you after the meeting and informs you that the 'Kingston Agency Against Crime' has agreed to fund the leaflets and arrange distribution on your behalf. They state this should be achieved within the next week and they will let you know when it has been completed.

❖ 57, 242, 141, 224, 206, 131, 112, 74, 127

🗁 2A1, 1B11, 1A4, 4G2, 1B9

One week later you are performing foot patrol early in the morning, as per your beat plan, when the local post deliverer approaches you while you are on patrol in the Kingston Park area. They tell you that they have heard about the recent crimes as a result of your leaflets and they may have just seen something of interest to you, but they are not sure and may be wasting your time. You assure them that this will not be the case and any information is more than welcome at any time. The post deliverer explains that while they were delivering to the community centre this morning they saw some gloves, a screwdriver and what looked like a torch. The items appeared to have been left behind the outside store cabin at the rear of the community centre. The post deliverer thought that they looked suspicious and just wanted to let you know.

What do you know?
- That the leaflets appear to be working as the post deliverer knew about the recent crime problems in the area and is more aware.

- The items seen at the community centre may be connected with the recent crimes.

What do you need to know?
- Whether the items are still at the community centre.

- If the items are connected to the recent crimes.

How are you going to find that out?

- Visit the community centre and search the area for the items.

- Research the crimes/liaise with Investigating Officers to ascertain if the items are linked.

What next?

You contact communications and update them on your location and what has been reported to you in order for them to record this.

You visit the community centre with the post deliverer who points out the items to you. They are still in the same position as they were this morning when they were first seen at 7 a.m. behind the outside store cabin. The items consist of a torch, a pair of woollen gloves and a screwdriver.

You contact communications for a check on the crime details and you are informed that a screwdriver has been used to force the locking mechanisms on the sheds attacked. You know that the crimes have been committed during the hours of darkness and have taken place in garden areas that are generally not well lit. It is therefore probable that a torch may have been used. The items are hidden out of view at the back of the store.

Taking all these details into consideration it is reasonable to assume that the items may have been used to carry out the crimes.

What next?

The post deliverer is anxious to continue with the post round as they have a time deadline to meet. You obtain full details, name, address, date of birth and contact details/phone numbers for the post deliverer. You thank them for their diligence and assistance and state that you will be in touch to update them regarding any further action taken with the property. The post deliverer then continues with the round, leaving you at the scene with the property.

What do you know?

- The items are still in situ at the community centre.

- It would seem that the items could be connected to the recent crimes committed in the area.

- You have obtained full details of the post deliverer.

What do you need to know?

- If these are the only items hidden in the area.

How are you going to find that out?

- Search the surrounding area for further items.

What next?

You check the rest of the area behind the community centre, in particular the vicinity of the outside store. Lying next to a compost bin you see a supermarket carrier bag and it is obvious that there is something inside. You look inside the bag and see that it contains a small garden fork and trowel, a pair of gardening gloves and a roll of green garden string.

What do you know?
● Following your search of the area you have found more property which may be linked to the crimes recently committed.

What do you need to know?
● The procedures for dealing with the property.

How are you going to find that out?
● Refer to your initial training.

● Speak to colleagues/supervision for advice (use personal radio for this if required).

What next?
You can recall from your initial training that the police place any property they deal with into the category of either *found property* or *property other than found property (POFP)*. In either case the items should be seized and documented according to force policy then placed in a secure store. (The location of the store may vary from force to force.)

Found property is normally an item/items that a person may have found and handed in to a Police Officer. It is classified as found property when it is believed that the circumstances are such that the legal owner would have genuinely lost or misplaced the item.

Property other than found property (POFP) is where it is believed that the property in question has not been genuinely lost or misplaced. It could include items that may have been stolen, items that may be evidence of an offence, etc.

It is therefore quite easy to define that the property which you are dealing with in this scenario is property other than found property.

Now you need to decide what your options are in relation to dealing with the property.

Options regarding the property
● Leave the property where it is to await forensic examination.

● Ask the community centre caretaker to keep hold of the items for the time being, and if anyone comes to claim them, to let you know.

● Remove the property and follow the correct procedures for dealing with it.

● Use your personal radio to summon a Police Officer to the scene, as you will need them to deal with this.

What next?

In the circumstances you decide that it is not necessary to await forensic examination as the property appears to have been there for a while and has been open to the weather prior to you finding it. (This would lessen the chances of gaining forensic evidence from the items.) Always seek advice from a Crime Scene Investigator (CSI) if you are unsure.

It is not an option to leave the property, as you believe it may be connected to a crime and you need to ensure that it is safe and secure as it may be evidence.

You consider calling a Police Officer then decide that you do not need police powers to deal with this.

You decide to seize the property and take it to the police office.

Seizing property

When seizing property there are many details to consider. You should think, for instance, about forensics or the evidential value of recovered items. You need to maintain the condition and safety of items that may belong to another. You must also be aware of your own health and safety as well as that of others who may be handling the property. You also need to consider whether it is of any evidential value to have the property photographed in situ where it was found. In some cases this may be helpful to give others involved in the case an idea of the area or to verify that the property was in that position etc.

What next?

- Taking photographs of the property in situ is not really necessary – both you and the post deliverer can provide statements to verify that the property was where it was.

- When seizing the property you need to take into account that forensic evidence may exist. There may be fingerprints/glove marks present, screwdriver size and shape may be matched to damage at the crime scene, gloves may have fibre or material transfer that can be matched to the scene. Take particular care in how you handle the items and place them into separate and appropriate bags or containers as soon as possible to preserve any evidence that may be present and prevent any cross contamination. (Remember this type of evidence is not always visible to the naked eye.) Wear gloves to prevent your fingerprints being transferred onto the items.

- All property items must be individually assessed for any risk that they may have:

  - contamination – toxic, corrosive, bodily fluids, etc.

  - sharp objects – knives, needles, etc.

You decide that none of the property items pose a health and safety risk from the information that you have at the moment. After seizing and packaging the property you take it to the property store.

What do you know?
You have found and seized the property following the correct procedures and have brought it to the property store.

What do you need to know?
- Where/how do you store the property?

- What documentation do you need to complete?

How are you going to find that out?
- Seek advice from the relevant person: supervision, property clerk, Crime Scene Investigator, Police Officer.

What next?
You visit the property office and speak to the property clerk; you follow procedure and record the property details into the property other than found book/register. The property and book/register is then checked and signed as correct by a supervisor.

As there is a property clerk on duty at the time you then hand the property and completed documentation to them to be placed in the secure store. (If there was no property clerk present the property would be placed in the designated holding area.)

What next?
You contact the Investigating Officer via your personal radio and update them regarding what has been found and what action you have taken. They reply and state they will take over from this point and will inform you of any progress, thanking you for your assistance.

At this point you return to your high-visibility foot patrol, ensuring that you complete the areas outlined in your beat plan. When you have completed your patrol you return to your office to complete the relevant paperwork for the day's activities. This will include:

- Pocket notebook;

- Community intelligence report regarding property found and action taken;

- Updates to the beat profile.

The following day you are on duty at 8.00 a.m. preparing to commence foot patrol within the Kingston Park area as per your beat plan.

What do you know?
- Yesterday you found some property that may have been connected to the recent shed burglaries in the area.

- Procedures were followed and the Investigating Officers updated regarding what had occurred.

What do you need to know?

- Is there a connection between the property and the burglaries?

- What has happened in relation to the investigation?

- Is there an update that you can give to the victims or residents yet?

How are you going to find that out?

- Contact the Investigating Officers for an update on the property/investigation.

- Seek advice from the Investigating Officers/Community Sergeant as to what, if any, information can be given to the victims/residents.

What next?

When you check your e-mail system you find that the Investigating Officers have sent an update. The property has been identified as being stolen from one of the shed burglaries, the screwdriver has been linked to all of the shed burglaries and forensic evidence has been found that links the screwdriver and torch to the suspect. The person has been arrested and charged with all of the burglaries.

The victims have been contacted and informed of the progress. They are all happy with the police action taken.

❖ 57, 242, 141, 224, 206, 131, 112, 74, 127, 1, 33, 101, 216

🗀 2A1, 1B11, 1A4, 4G2, 1B9, 2C5

What next?

You contact the Community Sergeant and provide a full update. The Sergeant requests that you update the parish council clerk as to the case progress in order for this to be brought up at the next meeting as a reassurance item.

DECIDE ON ANY FURTHER ACTION REQUIRED

What do you know?

- The Sergeant wants you to update the parish council clerk, who in turn will inform local residents via the meetings what has happened in relation to the burglaries.

What do you need to know?

- What details exactly are you permitted to disclose?

How are you going to find that out?

- Seek advice from the Community Sergeant.

What next?

The Sergeant states that as the case has not yet been to court there are only certain details that it is advisable to disclose for the following reasons:

- The age of a person dictates in law what details can be disclosed.

- The person is in the eyes of the law only suspected of an offence, as they have as yet not been found guilty or not guilty of an offence.

- The police may not want certain information about the offence and the methods of an investigation to become public knowledge prior to the case being heard at court.

- If the suspected person lives locally, details being disclosed may lead to reprisals by local residents on the person or those connected to them.

There are many areas of the law and police procedure that may affect how much, if any, information is released by the police in relation to investigations. Examples of these restrictions within the law and police procedure include the Police and Criminal Evidence Act 1984, as amended by the Serious Organised Crime and Police Act 2005, and the Human Rights Act 1998.

Before disclosing any information in relation to ongoing or past investigations it is always advisable for all employees within the criminal justice sector to seek appropriate advice first.

What next?

Following advice from the Sergeant you visit the parish council clerk and give the following update:

> Following a programme of reassurance policing involving foot patrols, community liaison and crime prevention advice, a person has been arrested and charged with the offences of burglary that have occurred recently within the Kingston Park area.

The parish council clerk states that they will ensure this information is fed back to the residents/community and is included on the agenda at the next meeting.

One of the main duties/responsibilities of a PCSO is to carry out *high-visibility patrols* in designated areas, in order to improve public reassurance, increase street safety and reduce incidents of public nuisance.

Although this is just one example of a community issue that can affect the public feeling of safety, it has highlighted that effective foot patrol can have a vast impact on such feeling. As you can see from the scenario, if all of the agencies involved had worked in isolation then information would not have been passed on and there is a possibility that the successful result outlined may not have been achieved.

❖ 131, 112, 1, 33, 74, 57, 101, 206, 216, 141, 242, 127, 224

🗁 1A4, 1B9, 1B11, 2A1, 2C5, 4G2

Note: Behaviours 🗁1A4 and ❖141 should be covered in most circumstances as normal working practices.

Flowchart – Effective Foot Patrol

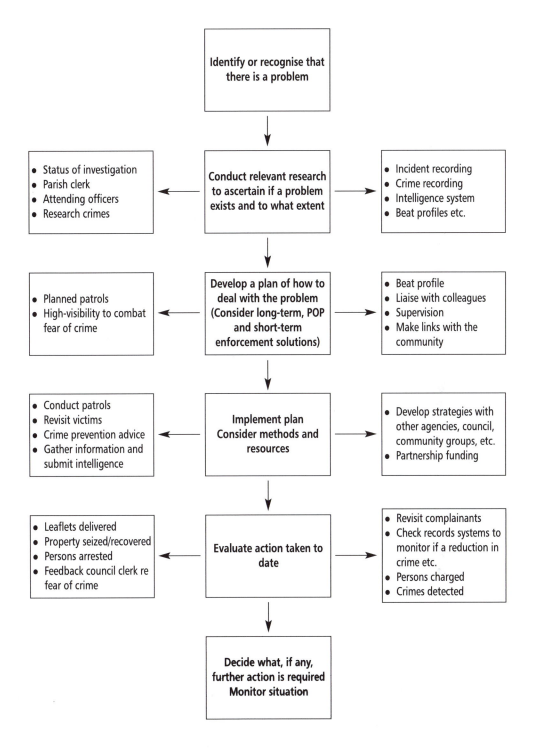

Identify or recognise that there is a problem

- Status of investigation
- Parish clerk
- Attending officers
- Research crimes

Conduct relevant research to ascertain if a problem exists and to what extent

- Incident recording
- Crime recording
- Intelligence system
- Beat profiles etc.

- Planned patrols
- High-visibility to combat fear of crime

Develop a plan of how to deal with the problem (Consider long-term, POP and short-term enforcement solutions)

- Beat profile
- Liaise with colleagues
- Supervision
- Make links with the community

- Conduct patrols
- Revisit victims
- Crime prevention advice
- Gather information and submit intelligence

Implement plan Consider methods and resources

- Develop strategies with other agencies, council, community groups, etc.
- Partnership funding

- Leaflets delivered
- Property seized/recovered
- Persons arrested
- Feedback council clerk re fear of crime

Evaluate action taken to date

- Revisit complainants
- Check records systems to monitor if a reduction in crime etc.
- Persons charged
- Crimes detected

Decide what, if any, further action is required Monitor situation

Chapter 4
Anti-social behaviour (youth nuisance)

This chapter covers criteria within the following units of the **National Occupational Standards** for Police Community Support Officers:

1A1 Use police actions in a fair and justified way

1A4 Foster people's equality, diversity and rights

1B9 Provide initial support to individuals affected by offending or anti-social behaviour and assess their needs for further support

1B11 Contribute to resolving community issues (PCSO)

2A1 Gather and submit information that has the potential to support policing objectives

2C4 Minimise and deal with aggressive and abusive behaviour

2C5 Contribute to providing an initial response to incidents (PCSO)

2C6 Contribute to planned policing operations (PCSO)

It is likely that the following **activities and behaviours** from the PCSO role profile will also be evidenced:

Activities:

131 – Adopt a problem-solving approach to community issues

112 – Conduct patrol

 57 – Use intelligence to support policing objectives

 69 – Prepare for and participate in planned policing operations

101 – Provide an initial response to incidents

216 – Complete administration procedures

242 – Make best use of technology

141 – Promote equality, diversity and human rights in working practices

127 – Provide an organisation response recognising the needs of all communities

224 – Work as part of a team

Behaviours:

- **Respect for race and diversity**
- **Team working**
- **Community and customer focus**
- **Effective communication**
- **Personal responsibility**
- **Resilience**

Introduction

Anti-social behaviour, in particular 'youth nuisance', has become a term used nationally within the policing arena. It describes incidents which generally involve a minority of youths whose actions or behaviour cause anxiety and fear for local residents or persons visiting an area. The government has implemented a Neighbourhood Policing Policy; this outlines that the PSCO has a responsibility to address anti-social behaviour issues. Due to the detrimental impact youth nuisance can have on communities it is almost always included within local policing objectives.

The scenario

Upon returning to work following a period of annual leave you are informed that you will be performing duties in the Fern Grange area. When preparing for your patrols you are looking to develop a beat profile. You check the communications incident recording system where you find that over the last two weeks there have been a large number of calls reporting youths causing a nuisance in the area.

IDENTIFY THE PROBLEM

What do you know?
There appears to have been a problem with youth nuisance/disorder in the Fern Grange area over the last two weeks and there have been numerous calls from the public reporting this.

What do you need to know?
- What are the details of the actual complaints?

- Who has made the complaints?

- What action has been taken regarding this problem to date?

- Has this type of incident occurred in the area previously?

How are you going to find that out?

- Check the communications systems for details of the complaints, caller details and action taken.

- Speak to the local Beat Officer/Community Sergeant for information regarding action taken and any history of similar events that may have happened in the past.

What next?

- Check the communications systems required to get the necessary information.

- Liaise with the local Beat Officer to discuss the problem.

- Familiarise yourself with the area and begin a beat profile.

You ascertain from the incident recording systems that the incidents are happening on evenings and weekends and that it is local residents who live near the park who are complaining.

The Beat Officer informs you that this is a recurring problem in the area during the summer months of the year. There are groups of youths aged between 12 and 16 years congregating in the small park area behind the general dealer store causing a nuisance. They are currently collating information to try and deal with the issue and would welcome any help that you can give.

❖ 57, 242, 141, 224

🗁 2A1

RESEARCH THE PROBLEM

What do you know?

The incidents are occurring on evenings and weekends in the park area at the rear of the general dealer. Residents living near to the park are complaining that there are groups of youths hanging around the area. They are believed to be aged around 12–16 years and the Beat Officer for the area is aware of the problem.

What do you need to know?

- What are the youths doing that is causing the residents to complain?

- Who are the youths involved?

- What, if anything, has been done in the past to combat the problem?

- What has the Beat Officer got planned for the area?

- Is there any CCTV in the area?

How are you going to find that out?

- Speak to the complainants to find out what the youths are doing.

- Check to see if any youths are named on incident reports or intelligence reports, or if any names are given to you by the local residents.

- Ask the Beat Officer about past operations or initiatives that have been run in the area and if there is any CCTV coverage of the area.

What next?

- Revisit the complainants personally and gather any further information that they may have in relation to the actual actions/behaviour of the youths. Ascertain what time of the day the problems are occurring and if they know the identity of any of the youths involved.

- Check all previous documentation completed in relation to the problem or area and collate any relevant information.

- Arrange a meeting with the Beat Officer and find out exactly what the problems have been in the past, what action was taken and the results. Find out what the officer has planned to tackle the problem.

Upon revisiting the complainants you find out that the youths are gathering at the park between 6 p.m. and 11 p.m. in the evening, although the problem is worse during the weekend. The youths are noisy and they are swearing and shouting abuse at passers-by. There is litter all over the park area and damage has been caused to the play equipment with graffiti scratched onto it. When residents have asked them to quieten down and modify their behaviour they have been faced with foul language and verbal threats.

The residents now feel intimidated by this and no longer go out to speak to the youths. One resident tells you that they know two of the youths belong to a well known family that reside in the Fern Grange area and they give you the name of the family.

From the incident reports submitted previously you find that the calls have been dealt with by Response Police Officers. The calls are logged as 'all quiet on arrival, local youths seen and moved on, all in order'.

The Beat Officer confirms that in the past the problem has been dealt with on an ad hoc basis due to resources being directed elsewhere to deal with public order issues within the town centre at the weekend. There is no CCTV covering the area.

The officer feels that adopting a **Problem-Oriented Policing (POP)** approach is the only way to provide a long-term solution to the problem. They are looking to develop an operation around this and ask you if will assist them with this by collating evidence and seeking solutions.

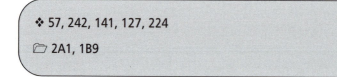

❖ 57, 242, 141, 127, 224

🗀 2A1, 1B9

DEVELOP A PLAN

What do you know?

The incidents are occurring between 6 p.m. and 11 p.m. mainly on weekends. The main complaints are excessive noise caused by shouting and swearing, as well as littering and damage being caused to the park equipment. When the residents have approached the youths they have been subject to abuse and verbal threats and are now feeling intimidated by the situation. It is believed that two of the youths involved are from a family in the local area.

There has not been a structured or planned approach to the problem by police in the past. Police have obtained no details of the youths involved as yet.

The Beat Officer wishes to take a **Problem-Oriented Policing (POP)** approach and has asked you to collate evidence and look for solutions to assist in this.

What do you need to know?

- What is Problem-Oriented Policing (POP)?

- How can you use POP to address this particular problem?

How are you going to find that out?

- During your training it is likely that POP has been covered. You may wish to revisit classroom materials/lesson notes or contact your force/local training department.

- Use computer-based learning/information programmes for police staff, e.g. Police National Legal Database, force intranet facilities, CENTREX websites for community policing issues and other internet sites.

- Liaise with colleagues/supervisors working in the neighbourhood-policing arena who are familiar with the process.

What next?

- You revisit your training notes and refresh your memory on the concept of POP.

- You liaise with the Beat Officer who guides you as to how to apply POP to this particular problem.

Problem-Oriented Policing

Problem-Oriented Policing (POP) is a guide designed to help you gather information quickly, evaluate it and make best use of the information in order to identify responses to policing problems.

POP focuses on specific crime and disorder problems with the intention of identifying the full problem and preventing the problem recurring in the future.

There are four main stages of POP, commonly known as SARA. SARA and POP have been used for some time as a methodical process for problem solving. It is a widely used tool within community/neighbourhood policing arenas.

The four main stages of **SARA** are as follows:

- *Scanning:* spotting problems by using knowledge and basic data.

- *Analysis:* using initiative and information technology to dig deeper into problems, their characteristics and underlying causes.

- *Response:* where a solution is devised, working with the community wherever possible.

- *Assessment:* looking back to see if the solution worked and what lessons can be learned from the process.

(Before embarking on a POP initiative always check to see if someone else has already tried to solve the problem. This could save you time and effort and help you to find out what worked and what did not).

The Beat Officer asks you to work from the SARA model and apply this to your problem.

What do you know?
- What the concepts POP and SARA are.

- The main stages of SARA and what is to be considered for each stage.

- The main issues regarding your youth nuisance/disorder problem.

What next?
You use the information you have to apply SARA to your problem.

You realise while you are applying the model to the youth nuisance issue that you have already covered some of the areas identified.

- *Scanning* – Spotting problems using knowledge and basic data.

This is the initial identification of the problem by effectively preparing your beat and checking the communications incident logging system. This led you to identify that a disproportionate number of calls had been received regarding youth nuisance in the area.

- *Analysis* – using initiative and information technology to dig deeper into problems, characteristics and underlying causes.

This is the use of information technology (checking computer systems) to obtain further information about the nature of the problem, details of the complainants, times and dates of occurrences, etc.

You have dug deeper into the problem and used initiative by speaking to complainants in order to get details of the youths involved. The actual behaviour and actions used that may be causing the problem have also been ascertained.

By finding out what action has been taken previously by both the Beat Officer and the officers attending the reported incidents, you have checked that you are not wasting time and effort on a problem for which there is already a solution.

> ❖ 131, 57, 69, 216, 242, 141, 127, 224
>
> 🗀 2A1, 1B11, 1A4, 2C6

What do you know?
- That by using best practice and researching your problem effectively so far, you have already covered the Scanning area and some of the Analysis area of SARA.

What do you need to know?
- How to complete the Analysis area of SARA.

How are you going to find that out?
- Visit the area at relevant times and gather evidence and information in order to identify characteristics of the problem.

- Speak to residents/youths and the community to establish possible causes of the problem.

What next?
- Arrange to conduct patrols in the area at relevant times when issues may be occurring.

- Make contact with residents/community members and the youths involved to try and establish some causes to the problem.

You visit the park area and find that the play equipment has been covered in scratched on graffiti. There is marker pen graffiti on the bench and seating areas. The surrounding grassed area is littered with empty cans and bottles, sweet papers and food wrappers.

The play area is situated within a large playing field and is not fenced off. It has a scruffy and uninviting appearance. The equipment within it is designed for use by small children. You notice that there are no litter bins in the vicinity.

The playing field is a well-used short cut to the local convenience store 'All Times'.

People are regularly walking past the play area going to and from the shop.

IMPLEMENT THE PLAN

What is your next course of action?
You commence high-visibility patrol in the Fern Grange area at 7 p.m. on Friday evening. It is around 7.15 p.m. when you reach the park area.

There is a group of six youths gathered around the equipment. They are talking among themselves and not causing any nuisance or disorder problems at present.

What are your options?

- Observe from a distance to see if the behaviour changes.

- Approach the youths, explain why you are present and build up a rapport with them if possible.

- Continue foot patrols, but not in the park area as there does not seem to be a problem.

What are your considerations?

- The youths have already seen you in the area so, if you observe from a distance, it is likely that they will be aware of your presence. This will affect their behaviour and will not give you a true reflection of the actual issue.

- If you are able to build up a rapport with the youths, you may be able to take the SARA model further by identifying why the problem occurs and what the underlying causes may be. You may also be able to establish the identity of the youths.

- Although there does not seem to be a problem at present (while you are there) you must not forget that is a recurring issue and it is highly likely that further complaints will made. If you recall from your initial research (Scanning) this is the policing approach that has been taken in the past and has not provided a long-term solution to the problem.

What next?

You decide to approach the youths.

You introduce yourself, and explain who you are, what you do and why you are in that particular area.

The youths are initially resistant but eventually with your persistence at making conversation begin to talk to you. They explain that they are all from the Fern Grange area and are happy to give you their details if you need them. You find out from them that not all of the youths that normally congregate are present tonight.

When you point out the state of litter everywhere they ask what they are supposed to do when there are no litter bins?

When you ask how the equipment has become damaged with graffiti, they respond by saying that it was definitely not any of them. They also refuse to give you details of who is responsible.

ACTION TO BE TAKEN

What do you know?

- The youths are congregating at the specified times in the small park area and they are all from the Fern Grange area.

- There has been damage (graffiti) caused to the play equipment. The youths present state they are not responsible for the damage and it appears other members of the group who are not present may have caused the damage.

- The youths have admitted they are responsible for the littering, but claim that there are no rubbish bins in the area.

What do you need to know?
- Why they choose to gather at that specific area.

- Does the behaviour ever become noisy/rowdy? If so, why?

How are you going to find that out?
- Ask the youths for their opinions on these issues.

What next?
- You ask the group the relevant questions using an open and friendly manner in order to keep the rapport that you have already built up.

They respond with the following;

1. They gather at the playing field as it is close to the shop where they buy food, drink and sweets. It is also central within the Fern Grange area so it is easy for everyone to get to.

2. The group is not really bothered about where on the field they go but the park area is the only place with any seating provided so they tend to gather around it.

3. Most of them meet up just to talk, listen to and exchange music on their MP3/iPod systems and buy items from the shop. One of them explains that sometimes some of the others (not present tonight) cause problems by being loud and cheeky to people as they walk past. They will not tell you who the others are as they do not want to 'grass them up'.

What next?
You inform the youths that even though there are no rubbish bins in the area it is still an offence to deposit litter and that they may end up in trouble for this. The shop has a rubbish bin outside that they may use or they can take their rubbish home with them and place it in the bin.

As you are talking you explain that this area is designed and intended for use by small children. The litter and graffiti does not make this a pleasant area for them to play in during the day.

On the whole the youths agree and confess that they do sometimes feel a bit stupid being in that area as it is for small kids. However, there are no areas designed for their age group and they get bored of an evening. They tell you that most of their age group used to attend the youth club, but it closed down a year ago as there were no adults who would run it.

While you are at the park you notice that some of the empty cans lying around have contained alcoholic drinks.

What do you know?
● The youths are gathering at that location because it is central, near to the shop and the only place with seating in the area.

● The lack of rubbish bins could be contributing to the littering problem.

● Alcohol is being consumed in the park area.

● It would appear that not all of the youths are causing the actual problems.

● Some youths may be responsible for the nuisance behaviour and damage caused.

● The local youths feel bored of an evening and state that they have nowhere to go and no facilities available for them in the area.

What do you need to know?
● Are other facilities available in the area for this age group?

● Is it possible to arrange for rubbish bins to be placed in the area and/or further seating to be placed around the playing field?

● The identity of the youths who may be responsible for the damage/nuisance.

● The identity of the persons consuming alcohol and where it is being purchased from.

How are you going to find that out?
● Liaise with the Beat Officer.

● Contact the relevant partnership/parish or council groups and ascertain what facilities are already in place, as well as what can be done to improve things if necessary.

● Contact local youth workers/groups to ascertain if any events, activities or clubs can be arranged.

● Visit the local shop and speak to the proprietor and staff to gain further information regarding youths and what they use the shop for.

What next?
● You arrange a meeting between yourself and the Beat Officer to discuss the progress to date.

● You visit the 'All Times' store in order to gain further information.

Before going to 'All Times' you check with the licensing unit and discover the manager holds an 'off-licence'. The store may therefore sell alcohol to be consumed off the premises. When you visit the store, the manager informs you that the youths visit the shop regularly of an evening and purchase sweets, food and drinks.

The manager assures you that the employees do not sell alcohol to persons under the age of 18 years and always ask for identification if they are unsure of a person's age. You explain about the problems that are occurring and the empty alcohol containers found in the park area. They state that they have never had a problem with the youths while they have been in the store and have certainly not sold any alcohol to the youths.

❖ 57, 69, 101, 131, 112, 141, 127, 224

🗁 1A4, 1B11, 2A1, 2C5, 2C6

What next?

You meet with the Beat Officer and provide an update regarding your progress to date. You decide the best way forward is to revisit SARA and see what stage you are now at.

- *Scanning* – you have already completed this area.

- *Analysis* – you had completed some of this, but you needed to identify characteristics and underlying causes of the problem.

By conducting high-visibility patrols, speaking to the youths and visiting the store you have identified certain characteristics. These are: people using the field as a short cut to the shop, certain youths causing problems, youths gathering in a small area, rubbish left, graffiti and damage caused.

You have also identified some possible underlying causes: lack of seating in the area, lack of facilities for young people aged 12–16 years in the area, no rubbish bins and possible consumption of alcohol by youths.

This area is now complete and you move on to the Response area of SARA.

- *Response* – where a solution is devised, working with the community wherever possible.

What next?
- You confer with the Beat Officer to discuss options of how to complete the Response area of SARA.

You explain during the meeting that from your findings so far you thought that perhaps the following might assist in providing a solution to the problem:

- provision of a rubbish bin in the area;

- provision of a further seating area situated on the playing field, but away from the short cut and park area;

- research into what facilities are available for youths in the area and introduction of new activities/facilities if possible.

The Beat Officer agrees with these suggestions and explains the lack of a rubbish bin or sufficient seating are part of what is known as **environmental factors** when dealing with a situation such as this. Environmental factors can form a large part of the problem.

What next?
You and the Beat Officer contact different agencies that fall under the umbrella of the 'Crime and Disorder Partnerships' and attempt to identify solutions. The agencies include the following:

- *Local council*. They agree to visit the park area and clean up the rubbish. They arrange patrols by neighbourhood wardens to monitor the littering and examine the graffiti on the equipment; if possible they will arrange removal or repainting. In conjunction with the County Council and Community Safety Units they will look into obtaining funding for a youth shelter.

- *Parish council*. They agree to look into funding for a rubbish bin and further seating in the park area.

- *Youth workers (Crime and Disorder Partnership groups)*. They agree to programme in visits to the area and conduct assessments of the facilities available for local youths. They will report back to the partnership with their findings.

What next?
You know that so far you have involved the community in providing some possible solutions to the problem. However, these are long-term solutions and will not provide any respite to the complainants who feel intimidated now and are looking for the police to tackle the problem.

What do you know?
The Beat Officer and yourself know that at present in relation to SARA you have achieved some of the Response area but you need to provide further solutions for the short term.

What do you need to know?
- Who are the youths that are causing the damage and being rowdy, disruptive and a general nuisance?

How are you going to find that out?
- Continue high-visibility patrols in the area at relevant times. This will also provide reassurance to the public.

What next?
- You plan out and conduct high-visibility patrols in the area at the relevant times.

While on patrol in the Fern Grange area on Saturday evening at 8 p.m. you receive a radio message reporting youths causing a nuisance in the small park area near to the shop. The caller wishes to remain anonymous for fear of reprisals.

You reply to the control room and inform them that you are in the area and are aware of the ongoing problem; you will attend the incident. You then make your way to the park.

> ❖ 131, 112, 57, 69, 101, 242, 141, 127
>
> 🗀 1A4, 1B11, 2A1, 2C5, 2C6

On your arrival you notice that most of the youths that you spoke to previously are present, but there are also others in attendance that you have not seen before. Two of the unknown youths are standing on the seat shouting to people as they walk past. As you approach them you notice one of the youths throw a soft drink can onto the floor. You inform control room of your arrival at the scene.

You ask the youth to pick up the can and he refuses. You warn the youth that he has committed the offence of depositing litter and request again that he picks up the can. He laughs and says 'no chance'. You then inform the youth that you are going to issue a fixed penalty ticket for the offence of depositing litter and he will be liable to pay £50 (approximately) or he can choose to be reported for summons. If a person is reported for summons their details are obtained and forwarded with a file of evidence for the offence committed to be put before a magistrates' court.

At this, the youth begins to comply and you take full details and complete the littering fixed penalty ticket. You also inform the youth that non-compliance with the terms of the ticket will result in an automatic court summons.

Your authority as a PCSO to issue a ticket will be dependent on the powers given to you by your individual force. If you do not have the relevant authority to issue the ticket then consider requesting a Police Officer's presence. The relevant County Council can administrate these tickets and a PCSO or Police Officer could be issuing them on behalf of the council. If this is the case payment details are outlined on the ticket issued.

In order to check his details and if there are any warrants, warning signals or other offences that may be outstanding you contact control and request a Police National Computer (PNC) check and an address check. You ensure that you are either out of hearing or wearing an earpiece when waiting for the check to come back to avoid the youths overhearing the result. The PNC check comes back: the youth is recorded not wanted, not disqualified and no warnings. The address check comes back correct to the details given.

As you are finishing with this process you see the other youth standing on a seat screw up a crisp packet and throw it at the can previously dropped. He then turns to you and states: 'He might be a wimp but I don't give a f--- what you lot say, what are you gonna do now hobby bobby?'

What is your next course of action?

You know by the demeanour of this youth that it is unlikely he will comply with your requests. You must consider your personal safety and that of others around you and also remember the limitations of your powers. You are working as part of the policing team and at times you will need to rely on the extended powers of your police colleagues. This includes situations where you are dealing with potentially confrontational/violent incidents such as this one. You contact the control room and request a police presence at the scene. It may be advisable to walk away from the group as you do this so that they do not hear what you say. This means that you can avoid the situation escalating any further prior to your assistance arriving.

You approach the youth and ask him to pick the crisp packet up. He replies: 'F--- off, you're not even a proper cop.' You explain the offence and the fixed penalty system again, and ask the youth for his name and address. He replies: 'Mickey Mouse, I live in a house with Minnie.'

At this the police arrive. You fully explain the circumstances to the officers and they approach the youth who immediately begins shouting and swearing stating that he will not give his name or pick up the litter. He becomes extremely agitated lashing out with his arms and making threats towards the officers. He is warned regarding his behaviour but continues and is arrested by the officers for a public order offence and removed from the scene.

> ❖ 131, 112, 57, 69, 101, 141, 127, 224
>
> 🗀 1A1, 1A4, 1B11, 2C4, 2C5, 2C6

What next?

You speak to the remaining youths and inform them that as you have been called to the park to deal with an ongoing incident you are asking them to account for their presence. It is necessary to obtain details from all the youths present and complete what is called a **STOP form**. (This is to comply with the Police and Criminal Evidence Act 1984 (PACE), Code of Practice A.)

When a PCSO/Police Officer requests a person in a public place to account for their actions, behaviour, presence in an area or possession of anything, a record of the encounter must be made and a copy given to the person who has been questioned. This record must identify the officer making the STOP and conducting the encounter.

The record must include:

- date, time and place of the encounter;

- if the person is in a vehicle, the registration number;

- reason why the person is being questioned;

- a note of the person's self-defined ethnic background;

- outcome of the encounter.

This is only required in the type of situation outlined above. STOP forms are not required for general conversations such as: giving directions, seeking witnesses or asking for general information to establish what has happened at incidents or disputes.

You obtain details from the remaining youths and complete the relevant STOP form for each youth. The youths are each given a copy of the form and the other copies are retained by you. The youths then disperse and go home for the evening.

You return to the office to complete the necessary paperwork.

What paperwork will you need to complete?
- In relation to the incident you will need to complete a full pocket notebook entry outlining what happened, what you actually witnessed and what your actions were. (Remember your pocket notebook rules.)

- The STOP forms will need to be entered into the register held within the relevant police office and signed by a supervisory officer.

- The beat profile will require updating.

- The arresting officers may require a witness statement from you covering the events prior to and leading up to the actual arrest as you witnessed this. (If this is not required at the time it will be requested later as it will be needed for the evidence file.)

- The fixed penalty notices for littering will need to be processed via whatever force or council system is in place. In relation to the person arrested this may be dealt with alternatively by the Police Officers in conjunction with the public order offence.

- You will need to update the control room regarding the initial call and what has happened.

- Any community or crime intelligence will need to be completed through the relevant systems and submitted.

What do you know?
- That you have now completed the Response area of SARA by providing short-term and long-term solutions to the problem.

What do you need to know?
- How to complete the final stage of SARA, the Assessment phase.

How are you going to find that out?
- Speak to Beat Officer/supervision and seek advice.

What next?
- You arrange a meeting with the Beat Officer to review the progress.

At the meeting with the Beat Officer you agree that the **Scanning**, **Analysis** and **Response** areas of SARA are now complete. To complete the final area, **Assessment** (looking back to see if solutions have worked and what lessons can be learned from the process) you decide on the following:

- For one month you will conduct checks of the communications logging systems and intelligence systems to monitor if any further calls are received and if the problem has ceased.

- For the next few weeks you will continue to conduct patrols at the relevant times in the area to monitor the situation.

- You will revisit the complainants and check how they feel the situation is at present.

DECIDE ON ANY FURTHER ACTION REQUIRED

You will arrange a meeting in one month to finalise SARA, if the problem has been reduced. In line with POP this community issue has been addressed using a multi-agency approach. For problems of this type it has been recognised that this is the most effective way to provide a long-term solution to youth nuisance/anti-social behaviour-related issues. This is because there are often underlying causes that require action as outlined in this scenario.

> ❖ 131, 112, 57, 69, 101, 216, 141, 242, 127, 224
>
> 🗁 1A1, 1A4, 1B11, 2A1, 2C5, 2C6
>
> **Note:** Behaviours 🗁 **1A4 and** ❖ **141** should be covered in most circumstances as normal working practices.

Flowchart – Anti-Social Behaviour (Youth Nuisance)

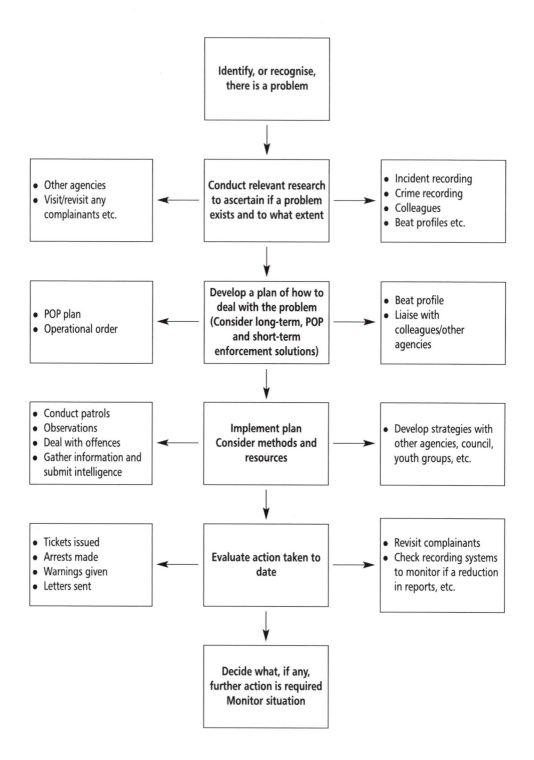

Chapter 5
Community meetings

This chapter covers criteria within the following units of the **National Occupational Standards** for Police Community Support Officers:

1A4   Foster people's equality, diversity and rights

1B11   Contribute to resolving community issues (PCSO)

2A1   Gather and submit information that has the potential to support policing objectives

It is likely that the following **activities and behaviours** from the PCSO role profile will also be evidenced:

Activities:

57 – Use intelligence to support policing objectives

216 – Complete administration procedures

242 – Make best use of technology

217 – Maintain standards of professional practice

141 – Promote equality, diversity and human rights in working practices

127 – Provide an organisation response recognising the needs of all communities

224 – Work as part of a team

236 – Participate in meetings

Behaviours:

- **Respect for race and diversity**
- **Team working**
- **Community and customer focus**
- **Effective communication**
- **Personal responsibility**
- **Resilience**

Introduction

Citizen-focused policing is a branch of the government's wider neighbourhood policing policy. It is defined as a way of working in which an in-depth understanding of the needs and expectations of individuals and local communities is routinely reflected in day-to-day decision making and service delivery. In order to hear people's concerns the police need to attend community meetings and ensure that the needs and expectations of people are recognised and appropriately addressed.

The inception of neighbourhood policing teams ensure certain officers/teams, either Police Officers or PCSOs, will have designated responsibilities for their local areas. In the past a Police Sergeant, or in some cases an Inspector, would have attended many of the meetings. This is no longer the case and where appropriate you will be expected to attend meetings as a representative of your particular police service.

The scenario

The Sergeant from your neighbourhood policing team has sent you an e-mail requesting that you attend West Leaf parish council meeting. The meeting is being held at 7 p.m., a week today.

The Police Officers from the team have had their shifts changed at short notice in order to police a football match on that day and no one else is available to attend.

IDENTIFY THE TASK

What do you know?
- You are required by the Sergeant to attend West Leaf parish council meeting and there is no one else to accompany you.

- The meeting is being held at 7 p.m. a week today.

What do you need to know?
- Where is the meeting being held?

- What is expected from you at the meeting?

How are you going to find that out?
- Speak to the Sergeant and obtain the information that you require.

What next?
You make contact with the Sergeant and ask where the meeting is and what is expected from you.

The Sergeant tells you that the meeting is usually held in the community centre on the High Street in West Leaf. However, you may want to check this with the clerk as sometimes when the community centre is in use the meeting is held in the church hall.

It is explained that you are attending the meeting as a representative of the police. It is expected that you will be prompt, polite and professional throughout. You need to report the outcomes of the meeting back to the Sergeant, as they are responsible for collating the information from all of the community meetings within the area.

RESEARCH THE TASK

What do you know?
• The venue of the meeting is not known for certain.

• You are required to report the outcomes of the meeting to the Sergeant.

What do you need to know?
• Where will the meeting be held?

• What is the format that you will use to report back to the Sergeant?

How are you going to find that out?
• Contact the parish council clerk and clarify the exact location of the meeting.

• Speak to colleagues, Beat Officers/PCSOs who have previously attended parish council meetings. Ask them in what format you need to report back to the Sergeant.

What next?
You speak to your colleague, an experienced PCSO, who explains that you are expected to complete a pro forma report following the meeting. This is the document that you forward to the Sergeant. You can obtain this form from the West Leaf parish council file, which is situated in the supervision office so that you can have access to it whenever you need it. They tell you that all of the relevant contact details for members of the council are also kept within the file.

At this point you ask the Sergeant for the file and obtain the parish council clerk's contact details. You take this opportunity to ask the Sergeant what is meant by 'be professional'. It is explained that you are attending the meeting as a representative of the police service as a whole, as the general public often do not differentiate between different forces and view the police as a whole organisation. They state they would expect you to prepare for the meeting, be prompt, polite and appropriate while attending the meeting and report the relevant information back to them in a clear and concise manner. As you are not previously known to the meeting they suggest you introduce yourself to the meeting on arrival.

You speak to the parish council clerk on the telephone and clarify that the meeting will be held in the church hall. You make arrangements to visit the clerk the following day.

DEVELOP A PLAN

What do you know?

- You need to fully prepare for the meeting.

- The meeting is being held at 7 p.m. in seven day's time at West Leaf church hall.

- You will be meeting the parish council clerk tomorrow.

What do you need to know?

At this point when asked to attend any meeting, the main question that you require an answer to is:

- **Do you actually need to attend the meeting?**

Police Officers and Police Community Support Officers are invited to attend a huge variety of meetings from community groups to forums. In order to ensure an officer's time is managed effectively and not adversely affected by attending unnecessary meetings, they need to know their actual presence at a meeting is required. Considerations could be given to alternative approaches to community meeting involvement that would achieve the same outcome in a more suitable manner and free up officer time.

The biggest waste of time is a meeting when it is not necessary. You would be surprised at how many meetings can be eliminated when you decide to meet only when it is absolutely necessary.

The following suggestions will help to guide you with this decision:

1. *Has a goal been set for the meeting?* Is there a purpose or goal to be achieved at the meeting? Every meeting should have at least one objective. If the meeting that you have been asked to attend does not have one, consider recommending other methods of communication, e.g. memo, e-mail.

2. *Has an agenda been created ahead of time?* An agenda is the basis for an effective meeting. This should be distributed at least one to two days prior to the meeting (preferably longer). It gives participants an opportunity to prepare for the meeting. Having an agenda during the meeting also focuses the discussion and helps the group stay on track.

3. *Will the appropriate people be attending?* If the appropriate people are not present then important decisions could get put on hold. It will also take time to update the individuals on what took place in the meeting they missed. It may be more productive to put the meeting on hold until the right people can be in the room.

4. *Could the information be covered/circulated in another manner?* The purpose of most meetings is to share information and update others. If possible make arrangements where appropriate to substitute your attendance at these types of meetings with an e-mail, memo or verbal update. Simply convey the relevant information in the agreed format to all of the people who would have attended the meeting. This will keep them up to date on what is happening.

Remember these are only suggestions to ensure that your time spent at meetings is managed effectively. Before you make any decisions to implement new procedures check first with the relevant supervision. There may be policies or protocols that have been agreed at a senior level between partnerships that will demand your attendance at certain meetings.

What do you need to know?
● Do you actually need to attend the meeting?

How are you going to find that out?
● Speak to the parish council clerk.

What next?
In order to clarify whether or not you actually need to attend the meeting you apply the previous suggestions:

1. Has a goal been set?

2. Has an agenda been created ahead of time?

3. Will the appropriate people be attending the meeting?

4. Could the information be covered/circulated in another manner?

You meet with the parish council clerk and introduce yourself. You explain your concerns and they provide the following information for you:

● All West Leaf parish council meetings have an agenda and full minutes are produced and circulated to all concerned following the meeting.

● All the relevant people will be attending the meeting.

● The meeting is held on a monthly basis, the purpose being to get the different parish councillors and partners together to discuss and address specific local issues. At other times, in between meetings, some information is circulated and suitable problems dealt with via other means. The actual meetings are an opportunity to share practices, ideas, responsibilities and funding for issues that arise within the specific parish.

What do you know?
● That it is appropriate for you to attend the meeting.

What do you need to know?
● What is your role at the meeting?

● Who else will be attending the meeting?

● What is the format of the meeting?

How are you going to find that out?
● Ask the parish council clerk for the details.

What next?

Now that you know that you are definitely attending the meeting, you ask the parish council clerk for the details of the other attendees, including information about their roles.

The clerk explains that the following people will be present:

- parish council clerk;

- elected parish councillors (one will probably be the chair);

- police representative;

- city/local council community safety/neighbourhood warden representative;

- members of the public;

- other invited interested parties (persons with specialist knowledge or a particular interest in an agenda item).

They tell you that these people perform the following roles:

- *Chairperson* (elected parish councillor) – will run the meeting and ensure that the agenda is followed and items are covered. They will also check the minutes that have been produced from the meeting and ensure that they are agreed as a true and accurate record.

- *Treasurer* (elected parish councillor) – will deal with budgets and funding matters and give updates on finances.

- *Parish council clerk/secretary* – will give any information on administration issues and background and provide any support that may be required. They will also undertake any tasks that are allocated at the meetings. They take notes, and produce and circulate minutes following the meeting.

- *Elected parish councillors* – will give their opinions, advice and decisions on all parish issues.

- *City/local council community safety/neighbourhood warden representative* – will report on any council-related issues and update the meeting about any current projects or information that may affect the council. Warden-focused duties and current action taken will be reported, e.g. dog fouling, littering and parking.

- *Police representative* – will provide updates on all policing issues in the parish area and any action taken, and inform the meeting about any projects or information that may affect the parish. As with all other attendees, the police representative needs to be prepared to answer any questions that may be raised.

- *Members of the public* – are allowed into the meeting. However, they are only allowed to contribute during the 'any other business' section.

The clerk explains that they will introduce you to the meeting at the start. They provide you with an agenda for the meeting and a copy of the minutes of the previous meeting.

WEST LEAF COMMUNITY PARTNERSHIP ASSOCIATION
PARISH COUNCIL MEETING

Meeting to be held on ----------------------- in West Leaf Methodist church hall at 7 p.m.

AGENDA

1. Welcome and introductions.

2. Apologies for absence.

3. Minutes of last meeting.

4. Matters arising from last meeting.

5. Policing update.

6. Local council/warden update.

7. Finance.

8. Correspondence.

9. Planning applications.

10. Any other business.

11. Date and time of next meeting.

NB. To all those groups who are hoping to hold an event during the year you are advised to check with parish council clerk, Davina Form (584 6678) who is the events co-ordinator and is keeping the parish diary. This will ensure that there are no double booked events as happened last year!

Chairperson --   Date -------------------------

WEST LEAF COMMUNITY PARTNERSHIP ASSOCIATION

PARISH COUNCIL MEETING

Minutes of meeting held --------------------- at West Leaf community centre at 7 p.m.

Attendance
Cllr Morland – chair
Mrs Form – clerk
Cllr Percival
Cllr Dixon
Mrs Carr
Mrs Snow – Neighbourhood Warden
PC Blair – Police
Mr Wynn (Safeplay – playground equipment)
Three members of public

1. Chair formally opened the meeting, welcoming all present and introducing Mr Wynn, new to the meeting as a representative of 'Safeplay' playground equipment to give a presentation during the course of the meeting.

2. Apologies for absence:
   Mr Bennett
   Mrs Jones
   Cllr Pye

3. The minutes of the meeting held -------------------- were approved and signed.

4. Police visit:

   PC Blair reported that there had been a theft from a motor vehicle at Tollgate fields, a report of criminal damage at Fair View (broken fence), broken windows at Front Street and School Avenue, burglaries at the Greyhound public house, School View and Leaf Gate. A serious assault had occurred in the Crescent and twelve reports of anti-social behaviour – youths causing a nuisance – had been received for the whole parish area.

   It was outlined that a policing surgery was being held in the community centre on ------------ ------- 4 p.m. until 6 p.m. where members of the neighbourhood policing team for the area will be available to provide advice and support regarding any policing issues. Crime prevention products and advice will be displayed and demonstrated.

   The officers left the meeting at 7.25 p.m.

5. Local council neighbourhood warden:

   Mrs Snow reported that at present the local park area is being monitored for dog fouling offences. This is following numerous complaints that have been received from local residents. To date one fine (fixed penalty ticket) has been issued in relation to dog fouling. It was explained that although this would appear to be a solution it is only one offender that has been addressed and there are still many others. Mrs Snow outlined that although she would continue to enforce this any offender had to be caught with the dog when the actual offence was committed. On the first occasion they would be issued with a written warning notice; only if they were caught in the act again could they be given a fine. Cllr Percival outlined that there were no dog fouling bins in the park area and Cllr Dixon (treasurer) stated that if the meeting were in agreement parish council were willing to part fund a dog fouling bin in the park. Clerk to make enquiries with local council and report back to next meeting.

   Chairperson --- Date --------------------------

6. Presentation – 'Safeplay playground equipment'

   Mr Wynn gave a presentation regarding the products that the company can provide for children's play areas. Chair thanked Mr Wynn and stated that should the council consider refurbishment of equipment within the parish area then the company may be considered.

7. Correspondence:

   WRVS donation request: Cllr Percival proposed £20, Mrs Carr seconded, all agreed. Letter from 'Green Group' re confirmation of the relocation of saplings at School Avenue.

8. Planning applications:

   3/06/000789 – Change of use and conversion of existing garage to residential bungalow with pitched-roof single-storey extension. Chelmer House, Front Street.

   Objections – Concern regarding access, essential bus stop, on a bend in road, dangerous.

   06/06/000710 – Outline application for residential development at former garage site to north of West Leaf Methodist Chapel.

   No objections.

9. A.O.B.

   Village in Bloom competition: agreed that we would take part this year. Cllr Morland to take the portfolio for this.

10. Finance:

   A quotation for repairs to pulleys for the church clock £653 plus VAT was received. The estimate was to be given to Rev. Buck for her comments and the matter to be further discussed at next meeting.

   It was agreed that any surplus cash at the end of the financial would be used for the provision of a bus shelter and further traffic calming measures in Leaf Gate.

   The separate finance budget sheet and balance was discussed and agreed.

The meeting was concluded at 8.15 p.m.

Chairperson -- Date -------------------------

By reading and understanding the meeting agenda and the minutes from the previous meeting you should now have a good idea of what the purpose of the meeting is and how it works. You notice from the minutes that following the police item on the agenda there are little or no other items that require your presence at the meeting. At the previous meeting the police representative left after their items had been covered. On checking this with the parish council clerk they confirm that you are not expected to remain after this item unless there is anything further that requires your input. (This is in line with the previous suggestions made for ensuring meetings are an effective use of your time).

What do you know?

- What the agenda and format of the meeting will be and what has been discussed at the previous meeting.

- Who will be attending the meeting and what their individual roles are.

- What your role is at the meeting.

What do you need to know?

- Any current local policing issues that may be relevant to the parish council.

- The information that you may or may not be allowed to disclose to the meeting.

How are you going to find that out?

- Ask the clerk if there are any issues that require following up from the previous meeting.

- Check the minutes of the previous meeting for any follow-up actions.

- Research intelligence systems.

- Research incident/crime recording systems.

- Speak to the Beat Officer/PCSOs for the parish area.

- Research any youth nuisance or beat profile documentation.

- Check if there are any current initiatives in place for the area, e.g. POP.

- Seek advice from supervision or the force Data Protection Officer regarding what you can disclose, to whom and when you can disclose it.

What next?

You have checked with the clerk and the minutes of the previous meeting and the pro forma report completed by officers attending the previous meeting. There are no outstanding issues from the previous meeting.

After researching the intelligence and incident/crime recording systems and looking at youth nuisance and beat profiles for the area, you obtain a comprehensive list of incidents that have occurred within the parish area.

Having spoken to the local Beat Officer you find there are currently no initiatives ongoing in the area. A Problem-Oriented Policing plan (POP) for youth nuisance around the local off-licence has recently been finalised.

You arrange to speak to the neighbourhood policing unit Sergeant and explain your concerns regarding the information you can disclose at the meeting. They look at the information you have and inform you that you may report any trends or unusual incidents. You may also tell them the number of crimes/incidents etc. that have occurred in the parish area. You must *not* disclose specific personal details, such as the names or addresses, of the people involved, suspects or victims, or any personal opinions that you may have on items that are discussed.

The disclosure of information may breach the terms of the Data Protection Act 1998 by which the police service is bound. Revealing personal information can also be an infringement of the individual's human rights and therefore be in contravention of the Human Rights Act 1998. Some of the incidents may be subject to further investigation and a criminal prosecution may arise from them. In this instance it is imperative the evidence is not disclosed in the wrong circumstances as this could compromise any further investigations.

Do not give your personal opinion on particular incidents or issues as it may be misconstrued that your opinions reflect those of the police service as a whole. It is therefore advisable to keep to the actual facts of each incident or issue and not be drawn into giving opinion.

> ❖ 57, 216, 217, 141, 224, 242
>
> 🗁 1A4, 1B11, 2A1

What do you know?
- The local policing issues that are relevant to the parish and what your update will be.

- The amount and content of the information that you are able to disclose to the meeting.

What do you need to know?
- Are you fully prepared for the meeting and ready to attend?

How are you going to find that out?
- Ask colleagues or supervision that have previous experience of attending these meetings.

What next?

You show the Beat Officer that gave you the information on the initiatives and incidents your preparation material. They reassure you that you are fully prepared and give you a *tip for the meeting*.

- Make sure all your material is collated into one summary to avoid having to flick through pages. This looks unprofessional and can be difficult to navigate.

IMPLEMENT THE PLAN

Now that you are fully prepared, you attend the meeting ensuring that:

- you arrive in plenty of time;

- you are smart in appearance and in uniform, if appropriate;

- you introduce yourself or are introduced to the meeting by another;

- you have all of your preparation materials required, e.g. agenda, minutes of previous meeting, research materials for your update.

During the course of the meeting it is important to be aware of the particular meeting rules and etiquette. Ensure that you:

- direct your comments, questions and answers through the chairperson;

- excuse yourself via the chairperson if you leave the meeting early;

- thank the meeting for the invitation to attend and any support, guidance or information that has been provided.

What next?

The parish council clerk introduces you to the meeting. You provide your update and information to the meeting. Following your input a question is raised from a parish councillor who asks if the police can address the problem of vehicles speeding along Front Street, West Leaf. They state that this is becoming a danger to other road users and pedestrians in the area and the problem appears to be getting worse.

You were not expecting this question and you are not sure of what the policing response will be or how you should reply to this.

If this occurs adopt the method that you have been applying during this chapter and ask yourself the following:

- What do you know?

- What do you need to know?

- How are you going to find that out?

- What next?

What do you know?

- The parish council has identified an issue regarding vehicles speeding on Front Street, West Leaf. It appears to be getting worse and is described as a danger to other road users and pedestrians.

What do you need to know?

- If there actually is a speeding problem in this particular area.

- Has it been identified as a problem in the past?

- Has there been any police action in the past?

- If there are particular times of the day, parts of the road, etc. where the problem occurs.

How are you going to find that out?

- Ask the parish council for full details of exactly when and where the problem is occurring.

- Research within the police service if the problem has been reported previously and what, if any, actions have been taken.

What next?

By applying the above system you now know that you are unable to give any firm response to this request. As you are not in full possession of all of the facts it is always prudent not to promise anything that you may not be able to deliver. Your actions should be as follows:

- Obtain as many details as you can from the people at the meeting regarding times and exact location of offences etc.

- Inform the meeting that you need to conduct further enquiries into the problem.

- Inform the meeting that you will ensure that this problem is researched.

- Reassure the meeting that you will reply to this request as soon as possible. If you can do this prior to the next meeting you will inform the clerk of any update. In any case a full update will be given at the next meeting.

- Ensure that you have left your full contact details with the council clerk.

By taking this approach you have ensured that you have obtained all the information required to further research/investigate the problem.

Most importantly, you have not made any promises that you may not be able keep. (For example the meeting feels that this is a problem that needs action and you have stated that you will ensure that the offenders are dealt with. However, following a speed recognition device being used repeatedly in the area it is found that the majority of vehicles are not breaking the speed limit.) This would limit the police response that can be given and could lower public confidence in the police.

The meeting is happy with your response and thank you for your input. You excuse yourself and thank them for the opportunity to attend.

> ❖ 57, 216, 217, 141, 224, 127, 236
>
> 🗀 1A4, 1B11, 2A1

EVALUATE THE COMPLETED TASK

What do you know?
- You have attended the meeting and provided them with an update as well as answering the questions asked in a suitable manner.

What do you need to know?
- How to record the outcomes of the meeting and who to forward it to.

- How to ensure the speeding issue is progressed and feedback given to the meeting.

How are you going to find that out?
- Obtain a pro forma from the West Leaf parish council file that you know is to be used to provide feedback to the Sergeant.

- Speak to the supervisor/Beat Officer for the area and provide verbal feedback regarding the speeding issue. Ascertain how this will be progressed.

What next?
You obtain a pro forma report from the West Leaf file and notice that after each meeting the pro forma, copy of the agenda and minutes are placed in the file for future reference.

WEST LEAF PARISH COUNCIL MEETING

DATE HELD:

OFFICER ATTENDING:

INCIDENT REPORT GIVEN:

ITEMS OF INTEREST:

FOLLOW-UP ITEMS:

Signed ---------------------------   Date -------------------------------

Supervisor -------------------------   Date -------------------------------

---

You complete the pro forma report, attach a copy of the agenda and forward it to the Sergeant.

DECIDE ON ANY FURTHER ACTION REQUIRED

You speak to the supervisor and the Beat Officer updating them verbally regarding the outcomes of the meeting. The Beat Officer informs you that a local resident has identified the speeding issue previously, directly to them. This was a few months ago; some research has been conducted and the officer states that they will contact the parish clerk and update them on the issue. The Sergeant agrees this and the issue is allocated to the Beat Officer to investigate.

You telephone the parish council clerk and inform them that the Beat Officer will be following up the speeding issue and will update them regarding the issue. This may be an opportunity to request feedback on your performance at the meeting.

In the example used in the chapter you stepped in to cover for an absence. However, on other occasions you may well be the designated contact who attends the meetings on a regular basis. Whether it is a parish council meeting like the one you have just worked through or another type of meeting the main principles that you have just followed will apply.

> ❖ 57, 141, 216, 217, 224, 242, 127, 236
>
> 🗁 1A4, 1B11, 2A1
>
> **Note:** Behaviours, 🗁 **1A4 & ❖ 141** should be covered in most circumstances as normal working practices.

The following are some examples of meetings that you may be required to attend within your role. The list is not exhaustive and some of the terms used may differ slightly from those used within your specific force or local area.

Types of meeting that you may attend:

- parish council meetings;
- housing group meetings;
- partnership meetings for community safety issues;
- extraordinary meetings – held to try and help a specific issue at a specific time;
- problem-solving group meetings, e.g. ASBO (anti-social behaviour orders);
- area neighbourhood team meetings;
- policing intelligence meetings;
- agency meetings, e.g. Pubwatch, Shopwatch.

Main principles to follow:

- Always ensure that you actually need to attend the meeting.
- Make sure that you are fully prepared prior to attending the meeting.
- Introduce yourself or be introduced to the meeting.
- Conduct yourself in a professional manner taking notice of meeting etiquette.
- Check what information you are allowed to disclose during the meeting.
- Always stick to the facts.
- Do not make promises that you may be unable to keep.
- When asked questions and you are not sure of the answer, do not attempt to bluff. Apply the method shown (What do you know? What do you need to know? How are you going to find that out? What next?). Do not be afraid to say that you will need to seek further advice.
- Always leave your contact details and ensure that you feedback any information to the meeting that has been requested as soon as possible.
- Report outcomes of meetings in the correct format to the relevant people.
- Enjoy meetings and do not be afraid of the formalities. Do not forget that more often that not the purpose of a meeting is to share information or solve an issue. People are therefore looking to achieve some kind of result by working together.

Flowchart – Community Meetings

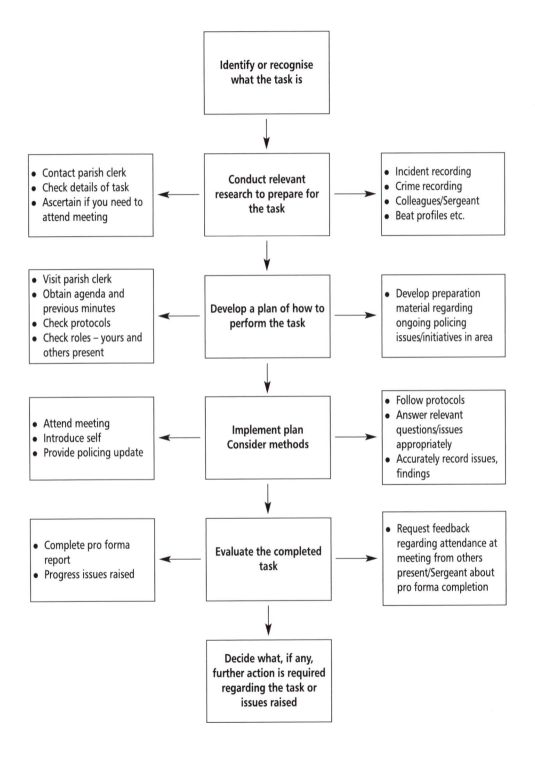

Chapter 6
Licensing

This chapter covers criteria within the following units of the **National Occupational Standards** for Police Community Support Officers:

1A1 Use police actions in a fair and justified way

1A4 Foster people's equality, diversity and rights

1B11 Contribute to resolving community issues (PCSO)

2A1 Gather and submit information that has the potential to support policing objectives

2C5 Contribute to providing an initial response to incidents (PCSO)

2C6 Contribute to planned policing operations (PCSO)

4G2 Ensure own actions reduce the risks to health and safety

It is likely that the following **activities and behaviours** from the PCSO role profile will also be evidenced:

Activities:

131 – Adopt a problem-solving approach to community issues

112 – Conduct patrol

57 – Use intelligence to support policing objectives

69 – Prepare for and participate in planned policing operations

101 – Provide an initial response to incidents

216 – Complete administration procedures

242 – Make best use of technology

141 – Promote equality, diversity and human rights in working practices

127 – Provide an organisation response recognising the needs of all communities

224 – Work as part of a team

Behaviours:

- **Respect for race and diversity**
- **Team working**
- **Community and customer focus**
- **Effective communication**
- **Personal responsibility**
- **Resilience**

Introduction

Many policing issues are currently linked to persons under the influence of alcohol and/or other substances. Where there are a concentrated amount of licensed premises in town and city centre areas, the problems with persons committing offences such as criminal damage, public order or assaults while under the influence of alcohol are apparent. They are also now invariably recorded on CCTV cameras installed in these areas. These offences are now becoming more and more frequent within other environments such as parks, villages, school playing fields, housing estates, etc. These types of offence affect not only the victims, but also anyone witnessing events, as well as the quality of life of residents within the area. Licensing laws are in place to try and regulate the sale and consumption of alcohol and the enforcement of these are the responsibility of the police and local council. This chapter will explore the practical issues behind some of the more commonly used legislation.

The scenario

You are responsible for the Fern Grange area, where you recall a couple of months ago you were dealing with an issue regarding youth nuisance/anti-social behaviour in the small park. A Problem-Oriented Policing (POP) approach was adopted, with many actions being taken from different agencies in an attempt to solve the problems. The amount of complaints received in the area almost stopped and revisits to the local residents indicated that the problem had improved significantly. It was highlighted through the police input that only a minority of the youths were actually causing problems. It would appear that over the past two weeks the problem is beginning to recur. Four calls have been received from different residents stating that youths are causing a nuisance in the park area and they appear to be drunk.

IDENTIFY THE PROBLEM

What do you know?

- There has been a previous issue regarding youths causing a nuisance in the small park area.

- A POP initiative has been implemented to attempt to solve the issue.

- The problem did improve but has now reappeared over the last two weeks. The youths involved now appear to be drunk.

- There have been four complaints over the past two weeks.

What do you need to know?

- If the problem has definitely returned and to what extent.

- Who the complainants are.

- What exactly the youths are doing.

How are you going to find that out?

- Contact communications, check incident logging systems and ascertain details of the complainants. Find out what was reported, times, behaviour, etc.

- Visit the complainants and find out what has been happening since the POP initiative began. Ascertain what impact this is having on them.

- Check the details and progress of the previous POP initiative including what actions were taken and what if anything is still outstanding.

What next?

When you check the communications incident recording systems you find that all of the complainants are from the houses that back onto the park area. The residents have all complained of youths congregating in the small park area. This is on most nights but particularly the weekends from 7 p.m. until 11 p.m. The reports state the youths are drinking, shouting and generally causing a nuisance.

When you visit the complainants they tell you that the overall nuisance problem has improved since the POP initiative was introduced. The youths have still been gathering at the park but have not been causing a nuisance and the littering and damage issues seem to have stopped.

They confirm that over the past two weeks the problem has started up again with youths becoming rowdy and abusive to passers-by. This is normally later on in the evening after 9 p.m. when some of the youths appear to be drunk. They feel alcohol is the main cause of the problems starting again and they are finding it intimidating to pass by or approach the youths.

The progress on the previous POP initiative has been going well and when you research this a little further you find the following:

- The local council has cleaned up the rubbish from the park area and removed the graffiti from the park equipment. The project for funding for a youth shelter is still ongoing in conjunction with the parish council.

- The parish council has provided funding for extra rubbish bins in the park area. These have been purchased and located in the area.

- Youth workers and the relevant partnership agencies are continuing with the project to increase facilities and activities in the area for youths.

RESEARCH THE PROBLEM

What do you know?
- The problem of youth nuisance does seem to be recurring in the area and it is linked to the consumption of alcohol.

- The complainants are local residents who feel the previous POP initiative did succeed in reducing the problem. The problem is in the early stages at this point and the residents are supportive of the police. They feel, however, it is beginning to affect their quality of life.

- The youths are OK until after 9 p.m. when they become rowdy and abusive. It is believed they may be drunk.

What do you need to know?
- What action the police have already taken in response to the complaints made over the last two weeks.

- What options may be open to you to deal with the current problem.

How are you going to find that out?
- By checking the computer incident records, intelligence systems and speaking to the officers who attended the initial incidents.

- Research your options by asking colleagues and supervisors for advice and guidance.

What next?
From the incident recording system you find that on two occasions the police have not attended until four hours after the initial report due to other ongoing incidents. This meant that by the time the police attended, it was into the early hours of the morning and the youths were no longer in the area. It was obviously too late to visit the complainants to obtain the full details and the sequels to the incidents on the logging system were recorded as follows:

Police attended scene, area searched, no trace of youths, all quiet on arrival. Too late to visit complainants, suggest ring back by early day shift.

On the other two occasions when the police had received reports the sequels read as follows:

Police attended area, youths made off on police arrival.

DEVELOP A PLAN

You arrange a meeting with the Beat Officer and supervisor for the Fern Grange area to discuss the options available to you. Between you it is agreed that you have the following options:

1. Do nothing, as the problem has not yet turned into a larger policing issue.

2. Continue with the core policing response that is already in place as there have only been four reports to date.

3. Reopen the POP initiative and adapt it in order to deal with the alcohol-related issues.

You all agree that you will use the POP approach in order to continue the significant progress which has already been made with the previous problem. You will reopen the POP initiative and attempt to remove the alcohol issue at this stage.

Problem-Oriented Policing

The benefit of using the POP approach to problem solving is, as you will recall from Chapter 4 on youth nuisance, that all actions taken and research completed is recorded. In a situation such as this, for example, when a problem reoccurs the process does not need to start from the beginning as you already have all of the previous details recorded. You are able to check the progress of the relevant areas dealt with initially, which will assist you with the new issue. Even if the POP process has been deemed completed you are still able to reopen it and add the new details in order to continue the problem-solving process. This ensures that you are not duplicating research into issues or actions that need to be taken.

What do you know?
- The police have given attention to the problem, however, a consistent approach has not been provided due to other policing commitments.

- You have different options available to you to deal with this problem. In consultation with the Beat Officer and area supervision you have decided that the most effective method to tackle the problem would be to reopen the POP initiative.

What do you need to know?
- What exactly is happening in the park area at the relevant times?

How are you going to find that out?
- Visit the area at the relevant times and observe for yourself.

What next?
The following Friday evening you arrange to conduct foot patrol in the Fern Grange area in order to give attention to the park between 7 p.m. and 11 p.m.

Personal safety/safety of others

You are planning to perform foot patrol in an area that is having problems with youths gathering, being rowdy and abusive. It is therefore possible there will be a number of youths present for you to deal with when you attend. There has been a suggestion that the youths are consuming alcohol. When people are under the influence of alcohol there is potential for them to behave in a violent or unpredictable manner.

Equipment and resources

As always, when you are preparing to commence patrol you must ensure that you have all of the relevant equipment with you. This may be full uniform, any protective or personal safety equipment that has been issued to you, personal radio and any paperwork/writing materials that may be required.

- In view of the previous considerations it would be advisable to ensure that you are not patrolling alone. The situation does have the potential to escalate into a public order situation.

- You will also need to inform communications where you will be and what the problems have been to ensure policing assistance can be sent to you quickly if required. Communications can forward details of any incidents reported regarding the problem to you as they are received.

- Inform the duty supervision and officers on duty where you are and what you will be doing in case you require police powers or assistance to deal with the situation. This will also help avoid the duplication of resources as the police officers will know you are already patrolling in the area.

> ❖ 131, 57, 69, 242, 141, 127, 224
>
> 🗀 2A1, 1A4, 4G2, 1B11

IMPLEMENT PLAN

What next?

You commence foot patrol at 7.30 p.m. in the Fern Grange location in company with your PCSO colleague. You are patrolling the park when you see a group of approximately six youths in the small park area near to the play equipment. They are talking and laughing among themselves and at this point do not appear to be causing a nuisance.

You approach the youths and see that a carrier bag containing cans of drink has been placed underneath the slide. Two of the youths appear to try and hide something behind their backs as they see you approach.

What do you know?

- There are six youths present at the park.

- The youths appear to be in possession of alcohol.

- Two of the youths are attempting to conceal something from you.

What do you need to know?

- The identities of the youths present.

- To whom the alcohol belongs.

- What it is that the youths are attempting to hide from you.

How are you going to find that out?

- Ask the youths who the alcohol belongs to.

- Request to see what the youths are hiding.

- Speak with the youths and ascertain their names and addresses.

What next?

As you approach the youths you concentrate on the two that appear to be hiding something. You ask the youths to remove their hands from behind their backs and show you what is in their hands. The youths comply with this and produce a bottle of cider that they were trying to hide. You note the cider has been opened and is only half full.

Your colleague checks the carrier bag underneath the slide and finds that it contains eight unopened cans of lager. You ask the youths who the alcohol belongs to but no one will answer you. They then state it was there when they arrived.

At this point you request the names and addresses of the youths present. Each youth is happy to comply with this and you write down the details.

What do you know?

- Two of the youths have in their possession bottles of cider that are opened and are only half full.

- There is a bag containing eight unopened cans of lager near to the youths.

- The youths are not willing to disclose to whom the alcohol belongs.

- The names and addresses of the youths have been obtained.

What do you need to know?

- If the names and addresses given are the correct details of the youths.

- How old are the youths present?

- If the youths have consumed any alcohol.

How are you going to find that out?

- Perform the relevant PNC (Police National Computer), and QAS (Quick Address Search) checks.

- In order to do the above checks you will require dates of birth that will then give you the age of the youths.

- Careful observations of the youths will indicate whether alcohol has been consumed.

ACTION TO BE TAKEN

What next?

You ask communications for QAS and PNC system checks on the details that you have obtained from the youths.

QAS check

The abbreviation QAS stands for Quick Address Search check. A QAS will provide you with the names of persons who currently reside at a given address. The information stored is gained from the electoral register. In most cases the details will be correct. However, it must be noted that, on occasion, the information may not have been updated recently (people may have moved house or not registered to vote). It may therefore be necessary to do further checks before deciding you are unable to ascertain or verify a person's correct address details.

Conducting the check

You request the check. When prompted by the communications operator you will provide as many details as possible regarding the address, house number, house name, full street/road name, village/town/city, postcode.

Result

The information will be returned by communications as:

All named persons currently registered at that address.

PNC check (person check)

The abbreviation PNC stands for Police National Computer check and will provide you with information regarding a person's previous convictions or cautions. It will also inform you of a last known address and last known description including any tattoos and identifying features. The PNC outlines if the person is currently wanted by the police and what for, as well as informing you of any current driving disqualification. Information is available regarding any warning markers that may relate to the individual such as drug user, weapons, violent, ailments, suicidal, self-harm, firearms, etc. This system will also outline if a person has been reported as missing from home or if an Anti-Social Behaviour Order (ASBO) is in force for an individual. Any bail conditions relating to a person will also be recorded. These areas are important and may affect how you decide to deal or communicate with a specific individual.

It is important that these checks are conducted for a variety of reasons. These may include the following:

- For your own personal safety, that of your colleagues or the public, and also for the safety of the individual. This may highlight the possible use of violence, or health and safety implications, like contagious diseases or drugs.

- To identify or confirm the identity of an individual.

- To ascertain if the person is wanted by the police. This could lead to action being taken by the checking officer that is different from what may have been planned when the check was requested.

- It may confirm that an actual offence is being or has been committed, for example driving while disqualified, or an offence that may relate to a previous conviction, such as the possession of a firearm following a prison term.

- To enable you to check if the person is breaching any bail/ASBO conditions.

Conducting the check

You request the check. When prompted by the communications operator you will need to provide the following details:

- call sign or collar number;

- location where the check is taking place;

- reason code for check (these are explained on your initial training);

- person's name, surname first then forenames;

- person's date of birth (do not use words such as fifty-eight, use digits such as 5, 8);

- person's place of birth (normally county or town such as Durham, Milton Keynes);

- sex of person (male or female);

- ethnicity description/code (such as White, Asian, Black, etc. – these are explained on your initial training).

Result

The information will be returned by communications as:

- confirmation of name and address, date and place of birth;

- whether the person is recorded or not;

- whether the person is wanted or disqualified;

- whether the person has warning markers;

- ASBO or bail conditions.

PNC is a national system used by all forces. It has a huge database and it is highly likely that there will be more than one person with the same name/details. It is important to ascertain as many details as possible for any search of the system.

The operator will not automatically give details of a person's previous convictions/cautions over the airwaves. This is for safety and security reasons.

The system is regularly audited and checked for improper use. There is a strict structure of how to conduct checks to provide an audit trail. A check will not be carried out by communications unless this structure is followed.

Other checks available on the system are driving licence checks for a person and vehicle checks (which now include insurance details).

If a person is not recorded on PNC this means they have not come to police notice for any of the areas previously outlined.

Personal safety

Ensure that you are careful how you obtain your reply from communications as this may dramatically affect the situation you are in and your safety. For example, if a person hears they are recorded as wanted etc. they may become violent or try to escape. Use an earpiece so only you can hear the results or, if an earpiece is unavailable, move away from the person being checked.

Know your local radio codes. They will indicate things such as:

- secure pocket set;

- double or single crewed;

- silent alarms etc.

(These will be explained during you initial training.)

Do not forget to use correct radio procedure and ensure that you use the phonetic alphabet to spell things or give vehicle registration numbers. This ensures that the message is clear and there is no confusion over details, e.g. N and M.

A – Alpha

B – Bravo

C – Charlie

D – Delta

E – Echo

F – Foxtrot

G – Golf

H – Hotel

I – India

J – Juliet

K – Kilo

L – Lima

M – Mike

N – November

O – Oscar

P – Papa

Q – Quebec

R – Romeo

S – Sierra

T – Tango

U – Uniform

V – Victor

W – Whisky

X – X-Ray

Y – Yankee

Z – Zulu

What next?

The communications operator replies with your check results. One of the youths you have checked is recorded on PNC, but they are not wanted or disqualified and there are no warning markers. The remaining five youths are not recorded. Five of the QAS checks come back as the details that have been given, but one does not match. You ask the youth if they have moved house recently and they state they moved eight months ago. You ask for the previous address and perform a further QAS check. This corroborates the details given.

As a result of the checks you now know that the youths are definitely aged 16 and 17 years of age.

While you are conducting the checks you ensure you are wearing your earpiece so that the details being given out by communications cannot be heard by others. Your colleague is talking to the youths and attempting to build up a rapport. When talking to the youths an officer can try and ascertain who has been consuming the alcohol. The main aspects to pay attention to are as follows:

• Can you smell alcohol/intoxicating liquor on a person's breath?

• Look at a person's eyes – do they appear glazed or staring?

• How is the person's speech? Is it slurred or difficult to understand?

• Is the person stumbling around or leaning on things to support them? Are they unsteady on their feet?

Although these are pointers to indicate a person may be drunk, unless you can smell alcohol or intoxicating liquor on the breath you must consider other reasons to explain a person's behaviour. They may be under the influence of drugs or have a specific medical condition. In this situation there is also the evidence of the half-empty alcohol bottles and full cans in the area that indicate that alcohol may have been consumed. You should also recall the previous reports of youths being drunk in this area at this specific time.

Using the above methods you ascertain that two of the youths in your opinion are drunk.

❖ 131, 112, 57, 69, 101, 242, 141, 127, 224

🗁 1A1, 1A4, 1B11, 2C5, 2C6, 4G2

What do you know?
• The youths are all aged 16 or 17 years (therefore none of the them have reached the legal age limit to purchase alcohol).

• Two of the youths appear to have been drinking alcohol.

• You have the correct names and addresses of the youths present.

• Only one of the youths is known to the police (PNC recorded). The youth is recorded due to a previous caution obtained for criminal damage. There are no warning signs, wanted or disqualified markers on this person.

What do you need to know?
• What powers you have to deal with the issue.

• What action you are able to take to deal with the situation.

How are you going to find that out?
• Refer to your training.

• Contact colleagues/supervisors for assistance.

• Request police assistance if required.

What next?

From your training you revisit the following legislation:

The Confiscation of Alcohol (Young Persons) Act 1997 was introduced to address the problem of under-18-year-olds drinking alcohol on the streets. This legislation has been amended on numerous occasions by the Licensing Act 2003, the Serious Organised Crime and Police Act 2005, the Police Reform Act 2002 and the Criminal Justice and Police Act 2001 to provide the following powers to deal with such situations:

- If a Police Officer (this includes a Police Community Support Officer) reasonably suspects a person in a *relevant place* to be in possession of alcohol and they are under 18 years of age, they may request the person surrenders anything in their possession which is alcohol or the officer reasonably believes to be alcohol or a container for alcohol. The person in possession of the alcohol/containers must also state their name and address when requested.

- If a person fails to comply with these requirements then they have committed an offence. The officer must warn them when making the requests that failure to comply is an offence for which they may arrested.

- Officers can seize *sealed containers*, as well as open containers and the intoxicating liquor they contain, and dispose of both in an *appropriate manner*.

Relevant place

- Any public place (other than licensed premises).

- Any place to which the person has gained access unlawfully (other than a public place).

Sealed containers

- An officer may only require a person to surrender a sealed container if they reasonably believe that the person is, has been or intends to consume the alcohol in a relevant place.

Appropriate manner

- The disposal of seized/surrendered items will be dictated by the individual force policies/protocols. You must ensure you are aware of what your force's disposal policies are. An example of a force policy could be that the items are disposed of in the presence of a supervisory officer and documented to that effect.

What do you know?

- The youths have been consuming alcohol and are in possession of opened and sealed containers of alcohol.

- The youths are in a public place (the park area).

- The youths are under 18 years of age.

- Due to the above you have the power to request them to surrender both the open and sealed containers and supply their names and addresses to you.

What next?

You make a formal request to the youths in possession of the alcohol/containers to surrender them to you. The request should cover the following points:

- I have reason to suspect that you are under 18 years of age.

- You are/have been drinking intoxicating liquor/alcohol/beer/cider, etc.

- You must stop drinking immediately (only if applicable).

- Please give me that can/bottle/container etc.

- What is your name and address?

- I must warn you that failure to comply with my request is an offence for which you can be arrested.

Do not forget to inform the person/s in possession of the alcohol/containers that action will be taken to dispose of the surrendered/seized items.

In these circumstances you have already ascertained and verified the names and addresses, so there is no need to repeat this.

The youths comply with your request and hand over the opened bottle of cider and the eight unopened cans of lager.

What next?

You know that at least two of the youths have been drinking and appear to you to be drunk. Although you have seized the alcohol, which will avoid any further consumption, you may still have child welfare issues on your hands.

In order to ensure the safety of these youths, as they are in a vulnerable situation, you request transport and escort the youths to their home address. This is to make sure they are safe and have someone to look after them until the effects of the alcohol have worn off. You also explain the circumstances to their parent/guardian to attempt to avoid repetition of this type of incident in the future.

The remaining youths are given advice following the complaints made by residents in the area. You suggest they return home and inform them letters will be sent to their parents/guardian regarding the incident they have been involved in.

What do you know?

- You have legally seized the alcohol/containers from the youths.

- You have taken two of the youths involved home to their parents/guardians and outlined the circumstances. The others have left the scene to return home at your request.

What do you need to know?

- How to dispose of the alcohol/containers that you have seized.

- What administration is required in relation to the action you have taken.

How are you going to find that out?
- Refer to your training.

- Seek advice from colleagues/supervision.

What next?
You return to the police office with the seized items and seek advice from the duty supervisor regarding your next actions. Following the advice you've received you complete an *alcohol seizure form*.

The title of this form and the person to whom it should be forwarded may vary from force to force. The form will generally include the following information:

- reporting officer details;

- date, time and location of seizure;

- reference number will be given if applicable;

- brief circumstances of the incident/seizure;

- age, date of birth, name and address of persons involved;

- items seized;

- method of disposal;

- signature of officer completing the form;

- supervisor signature.

You forward the form to the required persons in accordance with your force procedure. This could be the licensing unit, intelligence office or child protection team.

At present you are unaware of where the alcohol was purchased or who actually purchased it. This may be a significant factor in helping you solve the problem within the area so do not forget the need to preserve any evidence that may help you with this. The containers seized may carry a *bar code* on the packaging and this can be traced back to the store that sold the alcohol. If a bar code is present ensure you record the details in your pocket notebook and if possible remove/retain the packaging. Should the enquiries lead you back to a local off licence, for example, then you may wish to include this within the POP plan and deal with it in consultation with the Beat Officer/supervisor.

Disposal of alcohol

As previously outlined, the methods for doing this vary from force to force. If unsure seek advice. In this instance, the force policy requires the alcohol to be disposed of in the presence of a supervisor. The supervisor will sign the alcohol seizure form to confirm the disposal has been effectively carried out. The duty sergeant witnesses you pour the contents of the containers (sealed and opened) down the drain and signs the form.

You ascertain from a colleague who has dealt with a similar situation that you will need to complete the following paperwork:

- *Pocket notebook (PNB)*. Your PNB should be completed to include all relevant times, descriptions, details obtained, checks made, things witnessed by you, items seized and circumstances around this and actions taken. (Remember your pocket notebook rules.)

- *STOP form*. Obtain and check the details for each of the youths present (as in Chapter 4).

- *Intelligence reports*. Complete any community or crime intelligence through the relevant systems and submit.

- *Beat profile*. This will require updating.

- *Communications*. You will need to update communications regarding actions taken in order for the incident log to be completed correctly.

- *Licensing unit*. Depending on force systems you may need to inform the licensing unit, either the police, council or both of the incident and any actions taken. They can then collate the information, conduct further enquiries or assist you in relation to the enquiries regarding the purchase of the alcohol.

- *Youth nuisance letters*. For those youths who were not escorted home on the actual evening you may wish to send letters using official force documentation (most forces have drafts already in place) to inform the parent/guardian of what has occurred and the fact that the youth in their care was present at the time. These ensure the adults are informed of any police action taken and allow them to contact you or the rest of the policing team for further details if required. They may also act as a deterrent for the future and assist you in dealing with the longer-term problem. If you decide to use this method make sure that the letters are sent as quickly as possible after the event.

DECIDE ON ANY FURTHER ACTION REQUIRED

Make sure the POP plan is updated with the information gained and the actions taken in order for the problem to be reviewed. The residents/complainants should be informed of the police actions taken.

As you can see from the scenario, Problem-Oriented Policing can be used in many different ways and can even be resurrected to deal with a recurring issue. Tackling alcohol-related nuisance behaviour is a high priority within most forces and the duties performed by the PCSO can play a crucial part in the policing of these issues.

❖ 131, 112, 57, 69, 101, 216, 242, 141, 127, 224

🗁 1A1, 1A4, 1B11, 2A1, 2C5, 2C6, 4G2

Note: Behaviours 🗁 **1A4 and** ❖ **141** should be covered in most circumstances as normal working practices.

Flowchart – Licensing

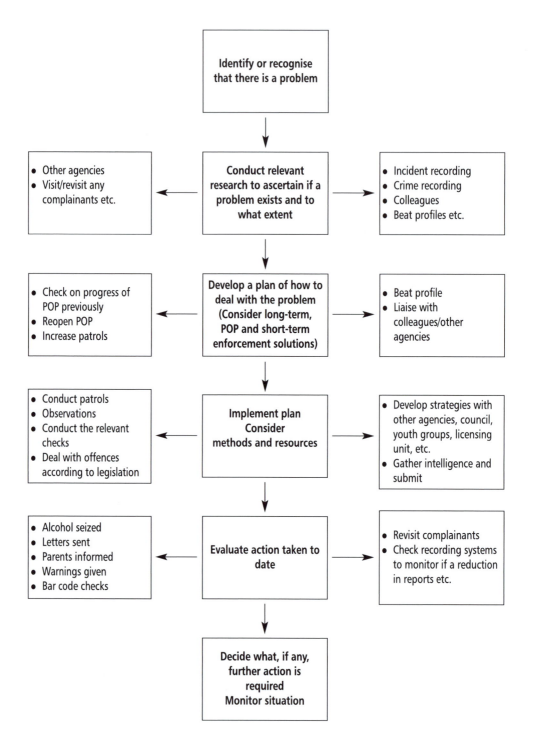

Chapter 7
Traffic-related duties

This chapter covers criteria within the following units of the **National Occupational Standards** for Police Community Support Officers:

1A1   Use police actions in a fair and justified way

1A4   Foster people's equality, diversity and rights

2C5   Contribute to providing an initial response to incidents

4G2   Ensure your own actions reduce the risks to health and safety

1E5   Contribute to road safety

1B11   Contribute to resolving community issues (PCSO)

2C6   Contribute to planned policing operations

It is likely that the following **activities and behaviours** from the PCSO role profile will also be evidenced:

Activities:

131 – Adopt a problem-solving approach to community issues

112 – Conduct patrol

115 – Respond to road-related incidents, hazards, offences and collisions

69 – Prepare for, and participate in, planned policing operations

101 – Provide an initial response to incidents

206 – Comply with health and safety legislation

216 – Complete administration procedures

242 – Make best use of technology

141 – Promote equality, diversity and human rights in working practice

127 – Provide an organisation response recognising the needs of all communities

224 – Work as part of a team

Behaviours

- **Respect for race and diversity**
- **Team working**
- **Community and customer focus**
- **Effective communication**
- **Personal responsibility**
- **Resilience**

Introduction

The increase in use of motor vehicles in our everyday lives has brought with it inherent problems for law enforcement agencies. With more vehicles on the road the likelihood of traffic-related offences being committed is increased. These may range from what are termed minor traffic offences, such as parking offences or document offences, to the more serious offences such as causing death by dangerous driving, or driving while under the influence of alcohol or drugs. During this chapter we will look at how to use road traffic legislation in a practical way focusing on how to deal with minor traffic offences.

The scenario

It is 9.30 a.m. on a weekday morning. You have just begun your tour of duty when you receive a radio message from communications. They inform you that there has been a complaint from a local resident regarding the parking of motor vehicles outside the shops on Front Street, West Leaf.

IDENTIFY THE PROBLEM

What do you know?

- A resident has complained about the parking near to the shops in Front Street, West Leaf.

What do you need to know?

- What time the call from the complainant was received.

- The details of the complainant.

How are you going to find that out?

- Ask the communications operator.

What next?

You acknowledge the call and make your way to Front Street, West Leaf. While on route the communications operator informs you that the call came in at 9.05 a.m. and the complainant is a Sam Berry, 28 Front Street, West Leaf.

What do you know?

- The call was received at 9.05 a.m. This is now one hour ago.

- The details of the complainant.

What do you need to know?

- If there is an actual problem with parking in the specified area.

- What is the extent of the problem.

How are you going to find that out?

- Visit the area and observe for yourself (as the complaint is happening now).

What next?

At 10.15 a.m. you arrive at Front Street. You notice there is a row of small shops on one side of the road. A zebra crossing is in place for pedestrians and a number of residential properties are interspersed with the shops. There are residential properties opposite the shops.

You notice there are motor vehicles parked on either side of the road and some are parked with two wheels on the pavement. The parked cars are restricting the width of the road and the traffic is therefore unable to pass without one party stopping.

RESEARCH THE PROBLEM

What do you know?

- There is a genuine problem regarding inconsiderate/illegal parking of motor vehicles in the area.

What do you need to know?

- How regularly this occurs – particular days, dates or times.

- Has it been a problem previously? How long has it been ongoing?

- What action, if any, has already been taken previously to tackle the problem?

How are you going to find that out?

- Visit the complainant and ascertain full details of what is happening.

- Speak to local residents/shopkeepers.

What next?

You visit Sam Berry, the complainant, who resides in a flat that is situated opposite the row of shops.

You want to obtain full details from him regarding the problem by asking him relevant questions to gain the information that you require.

Questioning

You need to use a type of question called an open question. This method of questioning is designed to elicit lengthy and full replies from the person being questioned. The opposite method, known as closed questioning, will encourage limited or one-word answers.

For example:

Closed question – Did you see a car?

Answer – Yes.

Open question – What kind of car did you see?

Answer – A blue coloured Vauxhall Astra.

As you can see from the example above, the use of open questioning does in general generate more information from a person. Open questioning is sometimes referred to as using 5WH. The reason for this is that most open questions include the words:

    Who – Where – When – What – Why – How   (5WH)

You apply 5WH when speaking to Sam Berry, asking open questions such as:

- Where exactly does the problem occur?

- What actually happens?

- When does the problem occur?

- Who do you think is causing the problem?

- Why do you think the problem occurs?

- How does it affect you?

- What has been done in the past to tackle the problem?

Sam Berry tells you parking is a problem everyday between 8.30 a.m. and 5.30 p.m., except Sunday when the majority of the shops are closed. He states people seem to park where they like in order to get as close to the shops as possible. They park on the pavement which means pedestrians cannot get past. Vehicles on the main road are unable to pass the parked cars as the road is partially blocked. The residents are sometimes unable to get in or out of their properties as parked vehicles obstruct the access routes. Although road markings are in place to show parking restrictions in the area, the drivers don't appear to take any notice.

Sam points out that the problem has been ongoing for the last two years and it has been reported previously to both the police and the council, but nothing seems to have been done about it.

What do you know?

- More details about the problem from the complainant.

- The effect the problem is having on the complainant.

What do you need to know?

- If the problem is affecting others and if so what the details are.

- What action has been taken previously with regard to the problem.

How are you going to find that out?

- Speak to the other residents and shopkeepers in the area.

- Check communications logs, incident records, beat profiles, etc.

What next?

You inform Sam Berry that you will be dealing with the problem. You explain that you will be in regular contact regarding any developments or information you are able to give. You obtain full contact details from Sam, such as full name, address, telephone numbers, e-mail addresses, etc. You leave your contact details should he need to contact you.

While you are at the location you decide to speak to other residents and shopkeepers in the area, using open questioning where appropriate. The shopkeepers say parking outside the shops is a problem in the area and at times it affects them. They are unable to receive deliveries as the lorries cannot get through due to the parked cars. They are concerned there is a need to have some sort of parking provision in the area for customers otherwise that may adversely affect their business.

When checking the incident records you find that there have been regular calls to the area regarding parking issues over the last six months and many residents have made complaints.

You visit residents who have previously complained. They all give you very similar information as Sam Berry. One resident tells you they are also concerned about the speed at which vehicles are travelling along Front Street as they approach the area of the shops. This is a 40 mph speed limit that then moves into a 30 mph limit at the shops. The resident tells you that vehicles do not slow down sufficiently to cope with the parked vehicles. They feel it is only a matter of time before an accident occurs. They have reported this previously to the police and recently to a parish councillor.

What next?

The incident records tell you that on most occasions the actions taken by police in response to complaints were to attend at the time (or as near to as possible), then give advice to drivers or issue fixed penalty tickets to offending drivers. You have checked the beat profiles for the area and found that there are no specific entries for this problem. On speaking to the supervisor for the area they tell you that they are aware of the problem but have only been able to send officers to deal with this as and when they are available. This has not been on a regular basis.

DEVELOP A PLAN

What do you know?

- All the residents questioned have similar complaints. One of the residents is also concerned about speeding in the same area.

- The problem has been reported to a parish councillor.

- The Area Sergeant is aware and has sent officers to deal with the problem; however, this hasn't been on a regular basis.

- The problem has been dealt with in the past by giving advice or issuing tickets.

- No beat profile entries exist for the problem.

What do you need to know?

- What has happened with the report to the parish councillor?

How are you going to find that out?

- Check the parish council file/records for the West Leaf area.

- Speak to the Beat Officer/PCSO who attends the meetings.

What next?

You check the parish council file for West Leaf and find that the speeding complaint was highlighted at the last parish council meeting. The PCSO in attendance has passed the information to the Sergeant who has allocated the problem to the Beat Officer to progress.

When you contact the Beat Officer they tell you the following:

- The Traffic Management Department from both the council and the police are looking at signs and road markings in the area to ascertain if they are sufficient.

- The Road Policing Unit has been asked to pay attention to the area whenever possible.

- A speed recognition device is due to be installed next week for one week. This device will produce statistics showing the number of vehicles actually speeding.

What do you know?

- That the speeding issue has been progressed and documented via the parish council and the Beat Officer.

- There have been problems in the past in the area with parking. Although the police were aware of the problem and some action has been taken, it has not been dealt with in a co-ordinated manner and the beat profile has not been updated.

What do you need to know?

- If the speeding and parking complaints can be linked.

- What action you can take to deal with the problem.

How are you going to find that out?

- Liaise with the police and council Traffic Management Departments.

- Speak to the area supervisor/Beat Officer to seek advice.

What next?

When you speak to the supervisor and Beat Officer it is agreed you will work on the problem alongside the Beat Officer. The speeding and parking complaints can be linked together and dealt with as one issue and the Sergeant suggests two possible approaches:

- *Short term* – use visible policing presence and enforcement to issue tickets for offences committed. This solution, while generally effective, is staffing intensive and can only be maintained for a short length of time.

- *Long term* – consider possibilities with regard to education, publicity and allocation of alternative parking facilities.

You begin a beat profile and at this point consider following a Problem-Oriented Policing approach (POP) as completed in the youth nuisance scenario. Remember, the principles of POP remain the same whatever the problem.

You contact Traffic Management and inform them of the parking issues within the area and the links to the speeding that they are presently dealing with. They state they will be happy to assist in any way that they can; however, they need to know what restrictions are already in place in the area. The unit says they will research this although it will take approximately 14 days for the reply.

> ❖ 112, 115, 101, 242, 141, 224
>
> 🗁 1A4, 2C5, 1B11

IMPLEMENT THE PLAN

What do you know?

- Both complaints from the area can be linked and dealt with together.

- The supervisor is happy for you to work with the Beat Officer to tackle this issue.

- You need a mixture of short and long-term actions to deal with the problem effectively.

What do you need to know?

● What the existing parking restrictions for the area are.

How are you going to find that out?

● Await the results from the Traffic Management Unit.

● Visit the area and record details of the restrictions already in place.

What next?

In consultation with the Beat Officer you both decide that two weeks to wait for the results from Traffic Management may unduly delay any short-term action that you can take. You conduct another visit to Front Street, West Leaf to record the restrictions that are already in place.

In order to keep the complainant updated while you are in the area you visit Sam Berry and outline the developments to date.

You remain in the vicinity observing the street from 2 p.m. until 3.30 p.m. While you are there the following incidents take place:

1. Vehicles are parking on the single yellow lines outside the row of shops. The occupants are then visiting one or more of the shops before returning to their vehicle and driving away. On most occasions the vehicles are parked for at least 10 minutes.

2. Delivery lorries are arriving and also parking on the single yellow lines outside the shops while they deliver goods to the shops.

3. Vehicles are regularly parked across the entrance to the residential flats situated opposite the shops. This entrance is marked on the road with 'NO PARKING, RESIDENTS ONLY'.

4. Vehicles are parking in the bus stop area while the occupants are visiting the shops.

5. One vehicle parked on the white zigzag road markings near to the pedestrian crossing while the occupant visited the shops.

What do you know?

● There are parking restrictions in place in the area in relation to:

  – single yellow lines outside the row of shops;

  – white road markings on the bus stop area and a marked bay with 'BUSES ONLY';

  – white road markings stating 'NO PARKING, RESIDENTS ONLY' on the driveway access area to residential flats;

  – white road-marking zigzags to indicate a controlled area for pedestrian crossing;

- concrete bollards situated on the edge of the pavement outside residential properties.

● The offending vehicles are usually driven by people attending one or more shops.

What do you need to know?
● What offences are being committed.

● How the offences can be dealt with.

How are you going to find that out?
● Research offences via books, journals, internet, force systems.

● Ask colleagues/supervision or training staff.

What next?
You confer with the Beat Officer and outline what you have witnessed and seek advice regarding the offences and methods of dealing with them.

The Beat Officer runs through each scenario in turn and gives the following guidance:

1. *Vehicles are parking on the single yellow lines outside the row of shops. The occupants are then visiting one or more of the shops before returning to their vehicle and driving away. On most occasions the vehicles are parked for at least 10 minutes.*

   This would be an offence of 'NO WAITING' as the single yellow line painted on the road means 'no waiting between certain times'. The signs situated nearby inform you of the allocated times when waiting is not allowed. In this case it is between 8 a.m. and 6 p.m. The legislation covering the offence is section 5(1), section 8(1) and section 53(5) of the Road Traffic Act 1984.

2. *Delivery lorries are arriving and also parking on the single yellow lines outside the shops while they deliver goods to the shops.*

   This would not be an offence as the restrictions on a single yellow line allow for the purpose of loading or unloading, as long as the time taken to achieve this is reasonable and not too long or the driver does not complete the loading/unloading and then leave the vehicle parked while they do something else. An example of this would be a lorry parked and delivering to the post office. This takes 10 minutes. The driver then leaves the vehicle parked in the same place while they go to the bakers to buy their lunch. As soon as the delivery is completed the vehicle should be moved or an offence of 'NO WAITING' would then be committed.

3. *Vehicles are regularly parked across the entrance to the residential flats situated opposite the shops. This entrance is marked on the road with 'NO PARKING, RESIDENTS ONLY'.*

   Although the road markings themselves are only a warning and cannot be legally enforced, if the vehicle is parked across the access route and is blocking the entrance/exit to residents and therefore preventing movement this is an 'UNNECESSARY OBSTRUCTION' offence. It does not matter if the flats are privately owned because the entrance/exit is a road. The legislation covering the offence is Regulation 103, Road Vehicles (Construction and Use) Regulations 1986.

4. *Vehicles are parking in the bus stop area while the occupants are visiting the shops.*

   This would be an offence of 'STOPPING ON A BUS STOP CLEAR WAY'. Where an area is marked/signed as a bus stop, parking within that area at any time is an offence. The legislation covering this offence is section 5(1), Road Traffic Regulation Act 1984.

5. *One vehicle parked on the white zigzag road markings near to the pedestrian crossing while the occupant visited the shops.*

   Vehicles are not permitted to park or stop on any of the controlled areas around pedestrian crossings. The white zigzag road markings found on either side of the zebra crossing signify a controlled area. Therefore in this instance an offence of 'STOPPING ON A PEDESTRIAN CROSSING CONTROLLED AREA' is committed. The legislation covering this is Regulation 20(2), Zebra, Pelican and Puffin Pedestrian Crossings Regulations 1997.

The Beat Officer then informs you that in the main these offences can be dealt with by the issuing of a *non-endorsable fixed penalty ticket.*

- A fixed penalty ticket is effectively the issue of a fine that is to be paid within a certain amount of time to the relevant force administration unit.

- 'Non-endorsable' means the offender is required to pay the fine issued. However, their driving licence is not endorsed with any penalty points as a result of this. This is due to the offence committed and the level of seriousness.

Scenario 5 is the only exception to this. Because of the more serious nature of this offence an *endorsable fixed penalty ticket* would be issued in this case.

- For endorsable fixed penalty tickets the fine imposed is higher.

- The fine needs to be paid but the offender also surrenders their driving licence in order for the relevant penalty points to be added.

A person can elect not to be dealt with via the fixed penalty scheme. They will then be formally reported for the offences that have been committed in order for a summons to be issued and then they will attend court on a given date in order for their case to be heard.

The Beat Officer then points out that the actual road markings and signs in Front Street appear faded and unclear. It looks as though they may have been there for a long time and have deteriorated with time and weathering etc.

In their opinion these restrictions may be difficult to enforce, particularly if the offenders challenge them, as they would have a justifiable defence of not being able to clearly see the restrictions.

What do you know?
- The offences that are being committed.

- The offences may be difficult to enforce due to the unclear/faded and weathered state of the road markings and signs in the Front Street, West Leaf area.

What do you need to know?
- What you can do to try and rectify this.

How are you going to find that out?
- Ask colleagues/supervisors/specialists, e.g. Road Policing Unit, Traffic Management Unit.

What next?
The Beat Officer and yourself arrange a meeting with the area supervision in order to seek guidance on your actions at this point. You provide the Sergeant with a full update regarding what has occurred so far. The Sergeant states that before you can take positive action about the problem by issuing tickets the road markings and signs will need to be clearly visible.

The Sergeant advises you to record your findings in a written report format to forward to the Traffic Management Unit in order for the relevant repairs to be arranged as soon as possible.

Following your visit to the area and the advice given by the Sergeant you compile the following report and forward a copy to the Sergeant, Beat Officer and Traffic Management Unit for their information and attention.

What do you know?
- The road markings and signs within the area are not sufficiently clear or visible for any legal enforcement to take place.

- The written report that you compiled has been forwarded to the Traffic Management Unit in order for the signs and road markings to be repaired or replaced.

What do you need to know?
- What other actions may be available for you to take to solve the parking issue.

How are you going to find that out?
- Ask colleagues/supervisors/specialists, e.g. Road Policing Unit, Traffic Management Unit.

Memorandum

From: PCSO 1111 Jones

To: Sergeant, West Leaf area, Neighbourhood Policing Team, Beat Officer, West Leaf Area Supervisor, Traffic Management Unit

Subject: Parking problems on Front Street, West Leaf.

Date: Today's date

I have examined the problems of illegal and inconsiderate parking in the area of Front Street, West Leaf, and following a site visit have come to the following conclusions:

- The regulation markings are in fact in such a poor state that only 20% of the restrictions can be legally enforced.

- The single yellow line, which runs the full length of Front Street from the bottom end of Coronation Terrace to the junction with Co-operative Terrace requires repainting as it is not fully visible.

- The area covered by the above single yellow line requires new supplementary 'No waiting during certain times' signs as the existing signs are weathered, unclear and the actual regulations cannot be read easily.

- There are two concrete bollards on the west side of Front Street outside a row of residential houses. If similar bollards could be placed outside the residential flats opposite the row of shops this may alleviate some of the obstruction issues that residents are experiencing.

- The bus stop bay on the east side of Front Street requires repainting and it would benefit from a sign being added in relation to no stopping at any time except buses.

This parking issue is also linked to a speeding complaint in the same area. If the traffic regulations were clearer and better defined this would make the enforcement of these regulations much easier and would ensure that the police service can deal effectively with the complaints made.

What next?

Having sought advice from your colleagues, you decide that in line with the POP model you have previously used you also need to look at some longer-term solutions to the parking issue.

While awaiting the results from the Traffic Management Unit you choose to continue your problem solving by looking at educating people with regard to the problem and the effects that it is having.

You endorse the beat profile with your actions so far.

You contact Sam Berry (the complainant) and provide an update on the action taken so far.

While speaking to Sam Berry regarding the education aspect, he states that he personally knows some of the shopkeepers and will ask if notices can be placed in their windows if it was thought that would help. He also offers to arrange the printing of the notices for you.

❖ 131, 112, 115, 101, 216, 242, 141, 127, 224

🗀 1A4, 2C5, 1B11, 1E5

ACTION TO BE TAKEN

What do you know?
- Sam Berry has offered to help you by printing 'No Parking' notices to display in relevant shop windows to help the problem until the permanent signs can be situated.

What do you need to know?
- Whether it is OK to use the signs.

- What other options may be available to you to tackle the problem.

- What alternative arrangements there are for parking in the area near to the shops.

How are you going to find that out?
- Seek advice from colleagues, supervision. (Don't forget to use the POP model to help you if necessary.)

- Ask the local council, parish council, shopkeepers and residents to ascertain if any other parking provision is available in the area.

What next?
The Area Sergeant thinks that the posters are a good idea and may assist the problem. They point out that they are for guidance only and you will be not be able to enforce them as they are not regulated signs.

After seeking advice from colleagues you formulate areas to progress while awaiting the results from the Traffic Management Unit regarding the signs and markings.

Using the POP model for structure and guidance you and the Beat Officer have provided the following responses:

- A visible presence has been provided in the area at the relevant times on a regular basis when the problem was occurring. High-visibility jackets were worn and residents, shopkeepers and road users were aware of the police presence in the area.

- The parish council and local newspapers were contacted and have agreed to include articles outlining the problems, action to be taken and areas for alternative parking. These will be for circulation in their papers and newsletters within the local area.

- 'No Parking' signs have been printed and displayed within prominent shop windows and within some residential property windows. Included on these signs is a direction to the car parking area.

- People that have been caught offending in the area have been stopped and given suitable advice regarding the offences that have been committed. They have been informed of the effect that these offences have had on local residents and the future enforcement campaign that will take place in the area.

- Where vehicles have been parked and left unattended and the offending driver has not been caught with the vehicle, details have been taken and recorded in Pocket Notebooks. A Police National Computer (PNC) check has subsequently been carried out to ascertain the current registered keeper of the vehicle and a pro forma letter pointing out the incident has been sent to the registered keeper.

Divisional Police office
West Leaf Section House
West Leaf
WST 2345R

This matter is being dealt with by PCSO/PC -------------- West Leaf Police Office, tel 0101 122 4445.

Date --------------------- Offending vehicle ------------------------- Registration no --------------------

Time --------------------- Offence committed --

Location--

Dear Sir/Madam

You are recorded as the registered keeper of the above vehicle. We believe that you and any others who may have use of your vehicle should be made aware of the difficulties currently being encountered by residents, traders and the general public in the above area in relation to inconsiderate parking.

I make no suggestions that you are directly involved. However, your vehicle was noted by police in the area potentially committing the above offence. This action results from many complaints from the public and is to make you aware of the road safety issues that are ongoing in the area at present.

This letter is for information only. However, legal enforcement of the parking restrictions will commence in the area shortly.

Should you have any queries or require any further information, please contact me on 0101 122 4445.

Yours faithfully

What do you know?

- What actions you are going to take to try and solve the problem.

- There is alternative parking in the area and it is suitable for people using the shops.

What do you need to know?

- When the road signs and markings are likely to be repaired or replaced.

- What progress has been made with the speeding complaint.

- How the complainant feels regarding the problem at present.

How are you going to find that out?

- Contact the Traffic Management Unit and request an update.

- Contact the Road Policing Unit for an update.

- Visit the complainant and ascertain if the problem has improved at all.

What next?

When you contact the Traffic Management Unit you receive the following update:

- Your letter outlining the problem with signs and markings has been forwarded to the Council Highways Department. It has been fast-tracked due to the dual problems of parking and speeding in the area and the possible road safety implications. The Council has replied and stated that they will carry out repairs as a priority.

- The results of the speed recognition device placed on Front Street have shown that only a very small number of vehicles were exceeding the speed limit. Therefore the problem does not warrant any further action from them and has been referred to the Road Policing Unit for information only.

You visit the complainant and update them on the situation to the present. They inform you that they are happy with this and relieved that some action is going to be taken at last.

Updating victims/witnesses/complainants, etc.

Whenever there is a complainant or victim involved throughout an investigation or policing problem it is important that they are updated on a regular basis as to what is happening. This will still apply even if there has been no particular progress. As well as being best practice and common courtesy, keeping people informed is now an obligatory task for the police service to perform. This is directed by the 'Victims Charter' which has been produced and circulated for use nationwide by those involved with the criminal justice system. The charter introduces guidelines and procedures for the police and other agencies to adhere to when dealing with victims/complainants. The levels of response required obviously vary due to different offences or the needs of individuals but the principles remain the same.

What do you know?

- The speeding issue has now been finalised.

- The signs/road markings will be repaired/replaced as a priority.

- The complainant has been kept fully appraised of the situation and is happy with the progress.

- The actions that you have chosen have all been successfully implemented.

What do you need to know?

- If the problem has ceased or improved at all.

- What progress has been made with the signs and road markings?

How are you going to find that out?

- Enquire with the complainant, residents and shopkeepers.

- Check recording systems, communications incident systems and beat profiles to monitor if there have been any further reports.

- Contact the Traffic Management Unit for an update.

What next?

The residents, complainants and shopkeepers tell you that, in the main, the problem has improved. However, there are still some people who are repeatedly parking in an inconsiderate manner.

The incident recording system and beat profile shows that there have been no further reports regarding the problem.

The Traffic Management Unit informs you that the Council will be repairing the signs and markings within the next few days.

What next?

To check on progress with the problem you attend the area the following week. On arrival you notice that the signs have been replaced and the road markings repaired. These are all now clearly visible. There is a considerable improvement in the parking and some vehicles are using the rear car parking area.

You notice an unattended vehicle that is parked across the access route to the residential flats opposite the shops.

What do you know?

- Repairs to signs/markings are complete therefore the restrictions can be legally enforced.

- The complainant, residents and shopkeepers are all happy with action taken. They feel that the problem has improved but there is still the odd vehicle causing problems.

- There is a vehicle parked across the access route to the flats.

What do you need to know?
- Details of the vehicle.

- What, if any, offences have been committed.

How are you going to find that out?
- Approach the vehicle and obtain the necessary details.

- Refer to previous training/research with Beat Officer.

What next?
You know that the vehicle is parked and left unattended and that it is blocking the access route to the residential flats. As you approach the vehicle a resident appears from the flats and points out that the vehicle has been there for 10 minutes and is blocking their vehicle access.

From the research that you conducted with the Beat Officer previously you know that the offence committed is 'unnecessary obstruction'.

Offence:

No person in charge of a motor vehicle or trailer shall cause or permit the vehicle to stand on a road so as to cause any unnecessary obstruction of the road.

The word *unnecessary* means that it must be an unreasonable act.

An *obstruction* is caused having regard to all the circumstances including length of time, the place where it occurred, the purpose for which it was done and whether it caused an actual, as opposed to a potential, obstruction.

The vehicle is a red-coloured Vauxhall Corsa, registration WE01 HHH. It has no damage to it and is secure. You make a note of these details and request a check of the vehicle on the Police National Computer (PNC) via your radio to communications. This type of check will give you the details of the registered keeper and any markers or reports that have been placed on the vehicle. Examples of these are vehicle stolen report, information markers such as obtaining driver details or vehicle believed involved in a crime, or DVLA markers such as vehicle not currently taxed, etc. The check on this vehicle comes back as a keeper from a local village and there are no reports or markers.

What do you know?
- The offence is unnecessary obstruction.

- The vehicle has no reports or markers on PNC, and it is registered as belonging to someone who lives locally.

What do you need to know?

- The options that you have to deal with this offence.

- The powers that you have to deal with this offence.

What next?

You know that you have the following options:

- Do nothing.

- Speak to the driver and give suitable advice.

- Issue a fixed penalty ticket.

It is for you to consider the circumstances, the definition of the offence and then use your discretion to decide which option you will take.

The resident from the flats tells you that they need to leave the flats in approximately two hours in their vehicle.

You have now been at the scene for five minutes and the driver has not yet returned. You decide that you will deal with this by issuing a fixed penalty ticket for the offence.

Note: If a vehicle is deemed to be causing an actual obstruction, or potential obstruction for road users in the future and is in a position or condition to cause obstruction or danger to others using a road, then the vehicle can be removed from that road to another place (Section 99, Road Traffic Act 1984).

In these circumstances you also have the option to have the vehicle removed. This would be performed via communications using the Force Contract Vehicle Recovery Scheme (CVRS). This will entail the vehicle being towed away and kept in a secure compound. The owner of the vehicle would then have to retrieve the vehicle and be liable for all costs incurred. If this were a circumstance where entry or access was required immediately then this option would be appropriate. However, it should not be forgotten that on occasion it might be a quicker option to conduct enquiries into locating the driver to move the vehicle and dealing with the problem via the issue of a fixed penalty ticket.

Powers to deal with offences

Depending on the individual force that employs the PCSO you may or may not have the power to issue a ticket yourself. If you are not in possession of this power this would be the point where you would summon the assistance of a colleague/police officer who would be able to assist.

As the driver is not with the vehicle you will be issuing the ticket and leaving it for the driver to intercept on return to the vehicle.

What next?

You need to complete the fixed penalty ticket fully and ensure that all details are covered. Before you start, ensure that you are using the correct ticket – remember that there are two types of fixed penalty ticket, endorsable and non-endorsable, according to the offence committed. In this case you will be issuing a ***non-endorsable fixed penalty ticket***.

Complete the fixed penalty ticket shown below in relation to the offence.

N/01287435

FIXED PENALTY NOTICE
(Non-endorsable offence)

UNAUTHORISED REMOVAL OR INTERFERENCE IS AN OFFENCE

Part 1

On __/__/_____ at/between ____ ____ and ____ ____ hours

In _____

_____

_____ a vehicle registered no. _____

Make _____ model _____ colour _____

Which you were driving/riding/using/in which you were a passenger/**which was unattended**, was seen in circumstances which gave reasonable cause to believe that the offence indicated below was being or had been committed.

Offence Code -/-/-/- _____

Signed _____ No _____ Area _____

Part 2   Title MR, MRS, MISS

Surname _____ Date of birth _____

Forenames _____

Address _____ Postcode _____

N/01287435

Excise licence serial no. _____

Expires _____

Issued at _____

A brief report must be recorded overleaf.

Do not forget that there is a rear of the form that must be completed. This is where you record your brief report outlining the offence committed.

IMPORTANT

REMOVE COPY TRANSFER SHEET BEFORE COMPLETING THIS PAGE

Note: The tickets are carbonated therefore they copy through to the page underneath in order for you to retain a copy of the ticket to forward to the relevant unit for administration purposes. Only the ticket that you retain has the rear completed. Therefore, as noted on the ticket above, ensure that you have removed the master ticket and you are not carbonating through to anything else when you are writing your brief report.

Also ensure that all the information has carbonated through to the bottom copy.

Take care when completing the ticket and be aware of your own personal safety. Where possible ensure that you are wearing high-visibility clothing. Avoid standing in the road - stick to the pavement. The tickets should be completed in black ink as this is easier for processing purposes such as photocopying.

You will note that on the ticket at Part 2, spaces are provided for name and address details. On this occasion these are not applicable. However, should the driver etc. be present then you would complete this. Compare your ticket with the following example:

N/01287435

FIXED PENALTY NOTICE
(Non-endorsable offence)

UNAUTHORISED REMOVAL OR INTERFERENCE IS AN OFFENCE

Part 1

On _15/09/2006_   at/between _1100_   and _1115_ hours

In _Front Street, West Leaf_ _____

_____

_____ a vehicle registered no. _WE01HHH_ ___

Make _Vauxhall_ _____ model ___Corsa_____ colour ___Red____

Which you were driving/riding/using/in which you were a passenger/**which was unattended**, was seen in circumstances which gave reasonable cause to believe that the offence indicated below was being or had been committed.

Offence Code _0/1/7/0_   _Unnecessary Obstruction_ _____

Signed _S Madsen_ _____ No ___0002_____ Area ___WL_____

Part 2   Title MR, MRS, MISS

Surname _____ Date of birth _____

Forenames _____

Address _____ Postcode _____

N/01287435

Excise licence serial no. ____013587832_____

Expires ___12/06_____

Issued at ___West Leaf_____

A brief report must be recorded overleaf.

IMPORTANT

REMOVE COPY TRANSFER SHEET BEFORE COMPLETING THIS PAGE

While on patrol in area following long-term complaints from residents about parking, I saw the vehicle, details overleaf, parked during the times shown. I saw the vehicle parked on the road unattended outside no. 33 Front Street, West Leaf. The vehicle was totally blocking the access driveway to the residential flats on Front Street. This would prevent any residents from entering or exiting the flats using a vehicle. I observed the vehicle for a period of fifteen minutes. No one returned to the vehicle during this time. The area is clearly marked on the road with 'No Parking Residents Only'.

One resident expressed concern regarding being unable to exit the flats with his vehicle. --

S Madsen PCSO 0002--

What next?

Once you have completed the ticket you need to place the original on the vehicle for the attention of the driver on their return. When you do this use the self-adhesive strip that is on the ticket to fix it to the windscreen of the vehicle so that it can be seen clearly. It is advisable to place the ticket underneath a windscreen wiper for extra security. Place it on the driver's side where it will be more visible to the driver on their return to the vehicle.

DECIDE ON ANY FURTHER ACTION REQUIRED

You will need to ensure that you have the full details for inclusion in your Pocket Notebook. A good tip is to use the information directly from the ticket, front and rear, to help.

You then submit the completed copy of the fixed penalty ticket through the relevant administration process within your workplace.

The POP plan and beat profile will need to be updated.

Although the powers to deal with vehicle-related incidents given to PCSOs currently differ greatly from force to force it is highly likely that the situations covered will be encountered in day-to-day duties. Vehicle nuisance and parking issues are high on the agenda in relation to offences that affect the quality of life of the people living within the areas affected. As highlighted in the scenario there are many different approaches that can be taken when dealing with this type of community problem.

❖ 131, 112, 115, 69, 101, 206, 216, 242, 141, 127, 224

🗁 1A1, 1A4, 2C5, 4G2, 1B11, 1E5, 2C6

Note: Behaviours, 🗁 **1A4 and** ❖ **141** should be covered in most circumstances as normal working practices.

Flowchart – Traffic-related Duties

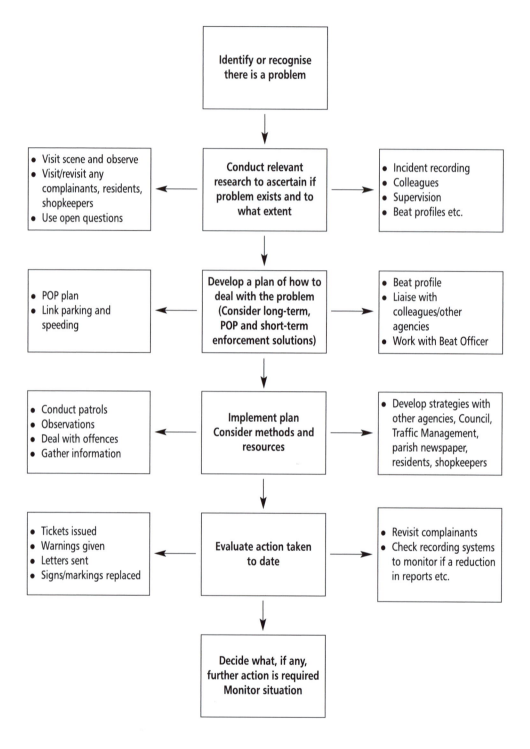

Chapter 8

Motor vehicle nuisance

This chapter covers criteria within the following units of the **National Occupational Standards** for Police Community Support Officers:

1A1   Use police actions in a fair and justified way

1A4   Foster people's equality, diversity and rights

2C5   Contribute to providing an initial response to incidents

4G2   Ensure your own actions reduce the risks to health and safety

1E5   Contribute to road safety

1B11   Contribute to resolving community issues (PCSO)

2A1   Gather and submit information that has the potential to support policing objectives

It is likely that the following **activities and behaviours** from the PCSO role profile will also be evidenced:

Activities:

57 – Use intelligence to support policing objectives

112 – Conduct patrol

115 – Respond to road-related incidents, hazards, offences and collisions

101 – Provide an initial response to incidents

206 – Comply with health and safety legislation

216 – Complete administration procedures

242 – Make best use of technology

141 – Promote equality, diversity and human rights in working practices

127 – Provide an organisation response recognising the needs of all communities

Behaviours:

- **Respect for race and diversity**
- **Team working**
- **Community and customer focus**
- **Effective communication**
- **Personal responsibility**
- **Resilience**

Introduction

The term anti-social behaviour is applicable not only to youth nuisance, but also to motor vehicles handled in an anti-social manner. Examples of motor vehicle anti-social behaviour include boy racers in car parks or the recent trend for using off-road motorcycles or electric scooters in residential areas.

The government has introduced a number of legislative measures over the past few years in response to this particular kind of anti-social behaviour. The Police Reform Act 2002, for instance, is one such legislation hoping to combat motor vehicle nuisance.

In this chapter we will look at how to put legislation into practice and focus on possible methods for dealing with a regularly encountered example of motor vehicle anti-social behaviour.

The scenario

You are on duty and conducting foot patrol in the West Leaf area at 6 p.m. on a Thursday evening. You receive a call from communications notifying you of a motorbike racing around on the school field at West Leaf Comprehensive. You are just around the corner from the specified location and inform communications you will attend.

IDENTIFY THE PROBLEM

What do you know?

- It's a Thursday evening after school hours and the school is closed. There is a report of a motorbike racing around the school field of West Leaf Comprehensive.

- You are nearby and will be at the scene in about five minutes.

What do you need to know?

- Who is the caller?

- Is there a description of the bike and the rider?

- Have there been any other recent reports of this nature in the area?

- Is this incident still happening?

How are you going to find that out?

- Recontact communications.

What next?

On your way to the incident you contact communications. They have been back in touch with the original caller and provide you with further information.

Communications tell you that the caller is watching the bike from her window, which backs onto the school, but at this stage she doesn't want a visit and wants to remain anonymous. All she can say about the bike is that it is a blue moped with a registration plate on it but she is unable to see the numbers. The rider is wearing a red helmet, a black T-shirt and blue jeans. She states that at present they are riding around in circles at speed churning the grass up and there are two other people watching. Communications tell you that this is becoming a regular complaint now, with six similar calls in the last week from other residents. There has also been a complaint from the head teacher at the school regarding the state of the field as a result of motorbikes using it.

RESEARCH THE PROBLEM

What do you know?

- The complainant is a resident whose house backs onto the school field. The caller wishes to remain anonymous at this stage. They are currently observing the moped and rider, so the incident is still ongoing.

- You have been given a description of the moped as blue, registration number is unknown, the rider is wearing a black T-shirt with jeans and a red helmet. The moped has been speeding around the field in circles churning up the grass. There are two other people in the area watching.

- This is becoming a regular problem with six other complaints in the last week from other residents. There is also a complaint from the head teacher at the school.

What do you need to know?

- Is it actually happening as the caller describes?

- What is the registration number of the moped?

- Is anyone else watching the incident? If so, do you need to consider personal safety or the safety of others? Could onlookers act as potential witnesses to the incident?

How are you going to find that out?

- Enter the school grounds and search for the moped, the driver and any onlookers.

- Observe/examine the moped and check the registration plate.

What next?

You enter the school grounds and approach the group with the moped. You notice that there is a rider and two other people.

As you enter the school grounds you see the blue moped skid to a stop next to the two other youths. You also note the moped has the registration plate NU05 LXT and is displaying 'L' plates. There are muddy circles in the field caused by the tyre tracks of the moped and as you approach you clearly request them all to stop there. This is done by using your voice in a loud and clear manner and using the relevant 'stop' hand signal.

'Stop' hand signal: hold your arm up at shoulder level, with your hand stretched out in front of you. Your hand should be facing upward with the palm pointing away from you.

They stop as requested and make no attempt to move off. (**Note:** The actual powers bestowed on you to request a vehicle to stop may differ from force to force. However, this would only become an issue should someone fail to comply with your request. Failure to stop would be a prosecutable offence and you would not be able to proceed without assistance.) **There is nothing to stop you requesting a vehicle to stop in these circumstances but remember, if in doubt, seek advice or request a police presence to assist.**

> ❖ 112, 115, 101, 206, 141
>
> 🗀 1A4, 2C5, 4G2, 1B11

DEVELOP A PLAN

What do you know?

- The blue moped has the registration NU05 LXT and you have seen it riding on the school field.

- It has now come to a stop next to the other two youths. There are bike tracks on the field where the moped has been. The youths have not made any attempt to run away or drive off.

(If they did decide to run or drive off, you would have to be clear and concise with the information to be passed over the radio: description and registration of the moped, description of the rider, direction of travel and possible area the moped may be heading to, if known.)

What do you need to know?

- Details of the bike and rider.

- Details of the other persons present and what their involvement is.

- What offences are being committed.

How are you going to find that out?

- Contact communications and conduct a Police National Computer (PNC) check on the registration.

- Speak to the rider and obtain their full details.

- Speak to the other persons present and obtain their full details.

- Refer to your training/knowledge regarding the anti-social use of vehicles. Consider what your powers are and what resources you may need.

Here is a short recap:

Section 59 of the Police Reform Act 2002 refers to vehicles that are being used in such a manner as to cause alarm, distress or annoyance to other people. A person can be warned regarding this and issued with a notice outlining this warning. If this warning is disregarded in a 12-month period the vehicle can be seized. You must have reasonable grounds that the vehicle is contravening either *section 3* or *section 34* of the Road Traffic Act *and* is causing, or likely to cause alarm, distress or annoyance to members of the public.

- *Section 3* – refers to someone driving a mechanically propelled vehicle on a road or other public place without due care and attention, or without reasonable consideration for other persons using the road or public place.

- *Section 34* – refers to a person without lawful authority driving a mechanically propelled vehicle on any common land, moorland or land of any other description that is not a road. This includes footpaths, bridleways and other restricted byways.

A PCSO has the power to enforce this legislation (if allocated by their Chief Officer). The only exception is that a PCSO has no power of entry into premises to enforce this unless supervised by a police officer.

What next?

You contact communications and request a PNC vehicle check on the moped registration number. You approach the youths and start to speak to them.

The result of the PNC check comes back as a blue Honda moped registered to a Christopher Dodds of 43 Springhead, West Leaf. Insurance details are held and there are no reports present. You speak to the rider of the moped and he confirms his details as the registered keeper. He gives his date of birth which makes him 17 years. The other two youths give their details as David and Andrew Dodds and explain they are Christopher's younger brothers.

IMPLEMENT THE PLAN

What do you know?

- The moped could be committing an offence under section 59 of the Police Reform Act 2002. It has been riding on the school field, which is not a road, and it has been driven in a way that has caused alarm, distress and annoyance to members of the public, hence the complaint.

- The rider and owner of the moped is a Christopher Dodds who is 17 years of age.

- The other two youths are Christopher's younger brothers, David and Andrew.

- There is current insurance for the moped.

What do you need to know?

- Whether the rider of the moped has *lawful authority* to be on the field.

- Confirm details of everyone present.

- Who is insured for the moped?

- Does Christopher Dodds have a licence to drive the moped?

How are you going to find that out?

- Ask Christopher if he has permission to be on the field.

- Ask communications to check the complaint by the head teacher to see if there is anything on the log that indicates whether anyone has authority to be on the field.

- Ask communications to do an address check on 43 Springhead, West Leaf to see which family live there.

- Check with communications who is down on the Police National Computer (PNC) as being insured for the moped.

- Ask communications to do a #DL check on the PNC. (This is a check to see if a person holds a licence and what they are entitled to drive. Details are recorded by the DVLA and placed on the computer. This helps officers when information is required to take immediate action regarding an offence.)

What next?

Christopher admits he doesn't have permission to be on the school grounds and was just showing off to his brothers. The school gate was open and no one was there, so he didn't think he was bothering anyone. Communications confirm that the past complaint from the head teacher of the school does outline that no one has permission to be riding on the school field. The address check shows that the Dodds family do live at the address of 43 Springhead, West Leaf and the PNC checks show that Christopher is the named insured person for the moped. He has the relevant licence to drive the vehicle and the moped also has a current road tax licence.

ACTION TO BE TAKEN

What do you know?

- You now know that Christopher does not have permission to be on the field, so he does not have lawful authority to be there.

- Christopher is therefore committing an offence under the Police Reform Act 2002, section 59, regarding anti-social use of vehicles.

- Christopher's details have been confirmed and all his documents are in order.

What do you need to know?

Under section 59 of the Police Reform Act 2002, a warning is issued to the person regarding the use of a vehicle in an anti-social manner before any further action is taken. You need to know if a warning notice has previously been issued to Christopher Dodds or the moped. A warning notice must have been issued previously in order for any further action to be taken in relation to this type of offence.

Note: The title of this warning notice will differ between forces. An example of this type of notice is the 'Traffic 183 Notice' and for the purpose of this chapter this is the title we will use.

How are you going to find that out?

- Contact communications to check the 183 notice warning file (or whatever the local checking system is called). Remember to request a check on both the person details and the vehicle details.

When a 183 warning notice is issued then details of both the person and the vehicle are recorded. This is to cover the type of scenario where a group of people may have been individually using the vehicle at different times or in different locations. This will stop a number of notices being issued to different people regarding the same vehicle and no further action being taken. In this type of circumstance a check on the vehicle details would highlight a previous notice being issued and this would have allowed further action to be taken.

What next?

You radio communications and they begin a check on the Traffic 183 file which is held on the computer and covers all persons and vehicles that have been issued with a notice. This will also tell you when the notice, if any, has been issued and who it has been issued to.

Communications get back to you after checking both Christopher's and the moped's details on the 183 file. It is a negative check, and this means they have not been issued a notice before. You now know that Christopher is eligible for a Traffic 183 notice, so you start to issue one.

You fill in all the details on the form, remembering to complete the form in an accurate and legible manner. When you issue the form give the person a warning, similar to:

You have been driving in a careless/inconsiderate manner, contrary to section 3 of the Road Traffic Act 1988…

or:

You have been driving on land, which is not part of a road/common land/foot-path/bridleway…

then add:

In a manner which is causing/likely to cause alarm, distress, or annoyance to members of the public.

I must warn you that if you continue to drive the vehicle in the same way or if you drive the vehicle on another occasion in the same manner within the next 12 months I can seize the vehicle under section 59 of the Police Reform Act 2002.

Request that the person sign the form (if applicable) to acknowledge receipt.

If a warning notice has already been issued within a 12-month period, you will need to take a different course of action. Under section 59 of the Police Reform Act 2002 you have the power to seize the vehicle.

- The vehicle will be recovered usually by the force contract recovery service that can be arranged by communications. A notice is issued to the person riding the vehicle explaining the seizure and where the vehicle will be removed to; a copy is provided to the recovery agent. The name of this form will differ from force to force and will be of a similar format to the seizure notice.

- What happens to the vehicle after it has been recovered may vary from force to force. A usual example of force policy is that vehicles are kept for seven days. The owner of the vehicle has to attend the recovery agent with full details of ownership for the vehicle and a valid insurance certificate for it. They will also have to pay a fee to remove the vehicle from the compound. If they fail to do this then the vehicle becomes the property of the garage and may be scrapped or sold at auction.

You issue the warning notice to Christopher Dodds and warn him regarding his conduct. He accepts this. You then request that he remove the vehicle from the school grounds by pushing it to avoid a further offence. He complies with this request. (By pushing the moped this means no further offences are committed. If he were to ride the moped then the offence would obviously continue to be committed.)

❖ 112, 115, 101, 206, 141, 216, 242, 127

🗁 1A1, 1A4, 2C5, 4G2, 1E5, 1B11

DECIDE ON ANY FURTHER ACTION REQUIRED

What do you know?

- Christopher Dodds has been issued with a warning notice.

- He has accepted this notice and has left the school grounds.

What do you need to know?

- What to do with the copies of the Traffic 183 warning notice.

How are you going to find that out?

- Ask colleagues/supervision to outline the procedure that you need to follow with the forms.

What next?

Colleagues tell you that one copy goes to the offender for their information, another copy is forwarded to the person/department who oversee vehicle recovery within your force area and the last copy is your copy. Your copy will usually be filed in the beat profile or intelligence file. The warning notice is usually a carbonated form so remember to take care when filling it in and make sure all the copies are accurate and legible.

Colleagues also tell you that it is best practice to complete an intelligence report regarding the incident remembering to supply the details of the vehicle and the offender. You should also explain where the incident occurred and at what time. This information could then be supplied to any off-road motorcycle section your force may have and the Beat Officer for the area so they become aware of the problem.

You need to inform communications of the actions taken and ensure that your pocket notebook is fully completed regarding the incident.

You also inform the head teacher of the comprehensive school of the incident and that a vehicle has been stopped on the school grounds and a warning notice issued. You advise the head that further attention will be given to the area to help combat the problem and ask them to report any further incidents of anti-social behaviour.

Vehicle nuisance issues are high on the lists of offences that affect the quality of life of the people living within the areas these incidents occur. Vehicle-related duties and road safety are an integral part of the PCSO role and the legislation recently introduced to help combat these offences provides a useful policing tool and should be used to good effect on a regular basis.

❖ 112, 57, 115, 101, 206, 216, 242, 141, 127

🗁 1A1, 1A4, 1B11, 2A1, 2C5, 4G2, 1E5

Note: Behaviours, 🗁 **1A4 and** ❖ **141** should be covered in most circumstances as normal working practices.

Flowchart – Motor vehicle Nuisance

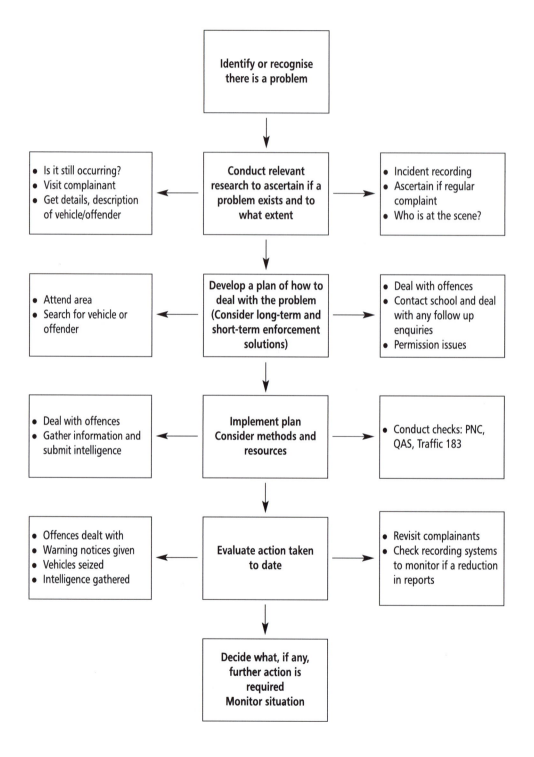

Chapter 9
Statement writing

This chapter covers criteria within the following units of the **National Occupational Standards** for Police Community Support Officers:

1A4   Foster people's equality, diversity and rights

2J3   Present information to courts or other hearings

It is likely that the following **activities and behaviours** from the PCSO role profile will also be evidenced:

Activities:

  42 – Prepare and present case files

216 – Complete administration procedures

217 – Maintain standards of professional practice

141 – Promote equality, diversity and human rights in working practices

Behaviours:

- **Respect for race and diversity**
- **Team working**
- **Effective communication**
- **Personal responsibility**
- **Resilience**

Introduction

Whenever a PCSO attends an incident, conducts a patrol or deals with any policing-related issue, there is a possibility that something may occur that could be of evidential value. This may not be apparent at the time but may come to light at a later date. If this happens then at some point a witness statement will be required to detail the events of the incident. A witness statement also highlights the skills of the officer completing the statement. Poor spelling or grammar and a lack of the required elements of the statement demonstrate an unprofessional image of the officer and the organisation. A missing or poor statement may eventually lead to an unsuccessful prosecution.

Using the scenarios you have worked through in the rest of the book, this chapter will take you through the process of preparing and writing a witness statement. The rules of statement writing will be covered and examples of completed statements provided.

The scenario

You report for duty and are checking your e-mails/post when you notice that there is a request from your Criminal Justice Unit (CJU) for you to provide a statement for inclusion on a court file. The request states that the case is *R* v. *Price*, burglary other, 28 Park Road, Kingston Park. The date of the offence is given as 'one month ago'.

IDENTIFY THE TASK

What do you know?

- A witness statement is required from you regarding an offence of burglary other.

- The offence happened at 28 Park Road, Kingston Park, one month ago.

- The case in question is *R* v. *Price*.

What do you need to know?

- When/where do you need to submit the statement?

- What you need to include in the statement.

- What was your involvement in *R* v. *Price*?

- Where will you find the information you need to complete the statement?

How are you going to find that out?

- Contact your Criminal Justice Unit (CJU) or the relevant department/person requesting the statement and ask for further information.

- Refer to your initial training on statement writing.

- Ask colleagues or supervisor.

- Check the relevant journals, documents or databases for information on what to include.

RESEARCH THE TASK

What next?

You contact the CJU, and the person requesting the statement informs you that you had conducted patrol in the area of the offence and recovered some property from the community centre. It turned out that some of the property was stolen property and other items were used to commit the offence of burglary.

They inform you they require the completed statement by the end of the week. The submission of this statement is subject to a time limit as the date of the court hearing is only two weeks away. You are asked to submit the statement directly to them.

You seek advice from your supervisor regarding where you will find the information you need to complete the statement. They advise you to look at all of the documents completed as a result of the incident. Your pocket notebook in particular should assist you with this.

You refer to your initial training notes on the subject of what to include in the statement and find the following guidance on the rules of statement writing.

<u>Rules of statement writing</u> (these rules apply to all statements that you will write):

- A witness statement form is a national form and is called an MG11.

- Remember to complete all of the boxes on the form. If you do not know and cannot find out all the information required remember to endorse the section *not known*. If the section is not applicable endorse the form *not applicable*.

- Any errors in the text should be ruled through with one line. The person making the statement should then initial the error. ***Do not*** use correction fluid or overwrite a mistake.

- Any additions to the text should be initialled.

- When setting out a statement, use paragraphs and ***do not*** leave blank lines. If you finish a sentence and there is a space at the end of the line consider whether you should rule off that line. (This is so that it cannot be alleged that you have added something later.)

- Try not to include opinion in a statement unless you or the witness is qualified to give it, e.g. expert opinion. Stick to the facts.

- Include your full name at the top of the form, with your SURNAME only in capitals. This applies to all names written in a statement, so that it is obvious which the surname is.

- After *occupation* insert 'Police Community Support Officer' and your number.

- Ensure that you complete the page number and number of pages section.

- Ensure that you date the statement.

- Your rank and collar number must always accompany your signature when you sign the declaration or any other part of the statement.

- When referring to timings you can use 24-hour clock or a.m. and p.m. You must follow the time with 'hours or a.m./p.m.' as applicable.

- Open the statement with the correct time, day, date and place. All PLACE NAMES must be in capitals.

- State whether you were in full uniform as this may be relevant for certain offences.

- You must describe the scene in as much detail as possible for the reader.

- When referring to other officers in your statement, use only their rank number and surname, e.g. PCSO 234 SMITH.

- Always write in black ink.

- Avoid abbreviations and police jargon in your statement. Write in plain terms so that everyone reading it can understand what you mean.

- Avoid writing *I would recognise the person again* or *I would not recognise the person again*. This may undermine the prosecution case if the circumstances change at a later date.

- Ensure when including names or places the spellings are correct. If you are not sure, ask!

- Sign at the foot of each page of text and after the last word of the statement. This is a requirement in law (Criminal Justice Act 1967 and Magistrates' Courts Act 1980). In the majority of circumstances, if a statement is not signed, it cannot be used in court.

- Relevant conversation needs to be recorded as direct speech. You should therefore reproduce the exact words used. Anything said by anyone other than a police officer or PCSO must be written in capitals.

- Avoid putting 'hearsay' evidence into your statements. In simple terms hearsay is something said other than 'in the presence and hearing of the accused'. This includes you writing in your statement what someone else heard if you did not hear it yourself. Hearsay evidence is not admissible in court. (If in doubt seek advice.)

- If you are describing someone or something in your statement make sure that the description is as comprehensive as possible. Describe a person fully including the following points:

  – colour

  – age

  – sex

  – height (use 'between' 5' 6" and 5' 10" heights, or 'about 5'8'" rather than a precise height)

  – build

  – hairstyle and colour

  – complexion

  – distinguishing features, e.g. marks, scars or tattoos

– clothing (from top to bottom)

– carrying anything.

- If you are not sure of a point of detail then you need to include this in your statement, e.g. *I am not sure of the colour of the woman's jumper.* This shows that you have considered the point even if you are unable to give details of it.

R v. *Turnbull*

The *R* v. *Turnbull* case highlights one of the main principles to consider when describing an incident in a statement. It is also a widely referred to case within police training and the criminal justice system. When dealt with in court the *R* v. *Turnbull* case highlighted a number of issues regarding witness statements and what should be included within a witness statement. The acronym **ADVOKATE** was derived from this case and indicates the following should be included in a witness statement:

A – Amount of time the suspect was under observation.

D – Distance between the witness and suspect.

V – Visibility: what was the lighting like, what were the weather conditions.

O – Obstructions to the view of the suspect.

K – Known or seen before: does the witness know the suspect; if so, how and when.

A – Any reason for remembering the suspect: this could be distinguishing features or peculiarities of the person, or the nature of the incident that made the person memorable. This can relate to previous or present sightings.

T – Time between the first and any subsequent identification to the police. This is not the time between first seeing the suspect and writing the statement.

E – Errors between the first recorded description of the suspect and his/her actual appearance.

DEVELOP A PLAN

What do you know?
- Which documents to use to give you the information that you require for your statement.

- The basic rules of statement writing.

- Where and when the statement needs to be returned.

- What your involvement was in the case.

What do you need to know?

- How to structure your statement and what to include.

How are you going to find that out?

- Ask supervision or colleagues for advice.

- Ask the CJU for guidance.

What next?

You speak to your supervisor who tells you to structure the statement chronologically and include everything you witnessed and the actions you took.

You now have an idea of where to start and you write your statement following the advice given and the rules of statement writing. The Sergeant gives you the following tips:

- Remember, if you are unsure of anything, seek advice.

- Once you have completed a statement and it has been accepted by the CJU remember to retain your copy. Keep this as a template to help you with any future statements that may be similar in content.

- If your handwriting is difficult to read and you must write in capitals all of the time, ensure any names, places, speech, etc. are underlined to distinguish them from the other text.

- The rear section of the statement must always be completed as far as possible.

IMPLEMENT THE PLAN/ACTION TO BE TAKEN

You have now completed the statement using the rules of evidence and guidance outlined (see Appendix C).

DECIDE ON ANY FURTHER ACTION REQUIRED

What do you know?

- You have written the statement as requested by the CJU.

- You have followed the statement writing rules and the tips given by supervision.

What do you need to know?

- Whether the content and structure of the statement are acceptable.

How are you going to find that out?

- Ask for advice from colleagues, supervision or the CJU.

What next?

You ask the Sergeant for advice on your statement. They tell you it seems fine and you are OK to submit it to the CJU. You copy the statement, keep a copy for your future reference and submit the statement to the CJU using the correct force procedures.

While you are photocopying your statement the Beat Officer from Fern Grange comes into the office and asks you to complete a statement in relation to the youth nuisance incident that occurred in the area as they are completing the case file.

Although the content of this statement will be different, the processes for preparing and writing a statement in general remain the same. You begin the process again, and prepare and complete the statement using the rules of evidence and guidance outlined (see Appendix D).

As the statement is different in content to the previous one you photocopy it and retain it for future reference.

What next?

The following day the Duty Sergeant hands you a request for a statement from the licensing unit. This notice informs you that they are going to proceed with a prosecution against an off-licence store in the Fern Grange area for selling alcohol to persons under 18 years of age. They require a statement from you in relation to an incident where you seized alcohol from a group of youths in the park area.

Remember the processes of preparing and writing a statement in general remain the same. You begin the process again, and prepare and complete the statement using the rules of evidence and guidance outlined (see Appendix E).

As you can see from the examples given, in order to write a witness statement you need to fully prepare and make good use of all of the documents you previously completed. These may include your pocket notebook, property forms, incident log entries, crime reports, any fixed penalty or other tickets issued, search, stop or seizure forms, etc.

The majority of the time the PCSO will be writing their own witness statements about what they have done, seen or heard, etc. The PCSO may progress to obtaining statements from other witnesses (this will depend upon the local force policy). If this is the case there are other issues to consider when obtaining this type of statement, and further training should be given in relation to vulnerable witnesses, Victim Personal Statements, etc. If a PCSO is asked to do this and is unsure then always seek advice.

Finally don't forget witness statements are evidential documents. The declaration found at the top of the statement form with a signature directly underneath will, if the circumstances permit, allow the statement to be served as evidence in the absence of the witness. It is therefore of paramount importance the statement is completed correctly, contains the relevant information in chronological order, is legible and follows the rules of statement writing.

Flowchart – Statement Writing

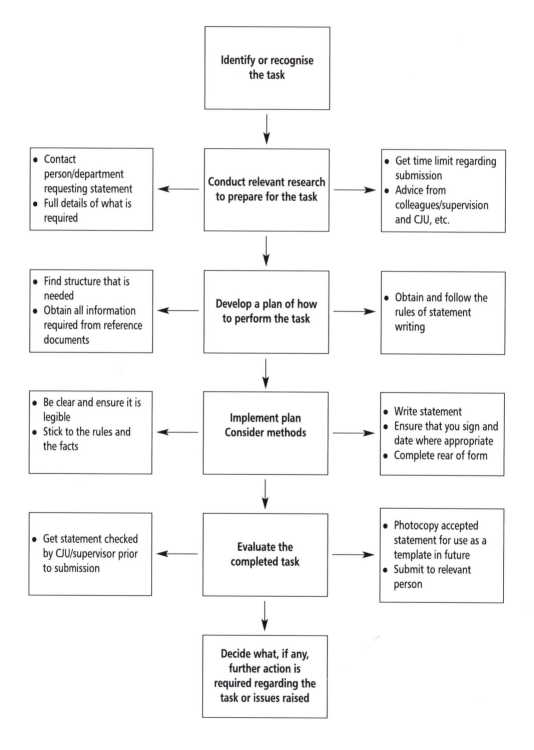

Identify or recognise the task

Contact person/department requesting statement • Full details of what is required ← Conduct relevant research to prepare for the task → • Get time limit regarding submission • Advice from colleagues/supervision and CJU, etc.

• Find structure that is needed • Obtain all information required from reference documents ← Develop a plan of how to perform the task → • Obtain and follow the rules of statement writing

• Be clear and ensure it is legible • Stick to the rules and the facts ← Implement plan Consider methods → • Write statement • Ensure that you sign and date where appropriate • Complete rear of form

• Get statement checked by CJU/supervisor prior to submission ← Evaluate the completed task → • Photocopy accepted statement for use as a template in future • Submit to relevant person

Decide what, if any, further action is required regarding the task or issues raised

Appendix A

PCSO: Suggested standardised powers

The power to:

1. Use reasonable force in the exercise of PCSO powers.
2. Require name and address for relevant offences.
3. Detain for relevant offences.
4. Deal with begging.
5. Require name and address for anti-social behaviour.
6. Require name and address for road traffic offences.
7. Confiscate alcohol in designated places.
8. Confiscate alcohol from persons under 18 years.
9. Confiscate tobacco.
10. Search for alcohol and tobacco.
11. Seize drugs and require name and address for possession of drugs.
12. Enter to save life or limb or prevent serious damage to property.
13. Limited power to enter licensed premises.
14. Seize vehicle that is being used to cause alarm to another.
15. Remove abandoned vehicles.
16. Stop vehicle for testing (s. 67, RTA 1988).
17. Stop pedal cycle.
18. Control traffic.
19. Direct traffic for the purpose of escorting abnormal loads.
20. Conduct road checks (authorised officer).
21. Place road traffic signs.
22. Enforce cordoned areas (terrorism).
23. Stop and search in authorised areas (terrorism).
24. Photograph persons away from a police station.

The power to issue fixed penalty notices as authorised by the Police Reform Act 2005:

25. For disorder.

26. For cycling on a footpath.

27. For dog fouling.

28. For graffiti and fly posting.

29. For littering.

30. For dog control orders.

The power to issue fixed penalty notices for disorder as authorised by the Criminal Justice and Police Act 2005:

31. For sale of alcohol to a person who is drunk.

32. For sale of alcohol to children.

33. For purchase of alcohol by or on behalf of children.

34. For buying or attempting to buy alcohol for consumption on licensed premises by a child.

35. For consumption of alcohol by children or allowing such consumption.

36. For delivery of alcohol to children or allowing such delivery.

37. For drinking in a designated public area.

38. For causing harassment, alarm or distress.

39. For destroying or damaging property (under £500).

40. For throwing fireworks.

41. For breach of fireworks curfew.

42. For possession of a category 4 firework.

43. For possession by a person under 18 years of an adult firework.

44. For supply of an excessively loud firework.

45. For trespassing on a railway.

46. For throwing stones on a railway.

Appendix B
PCSO: Role profile

Core Responsibilities	Activity no.	Activities The role holder should effectively deliver these key requirements
Community Safety	131	**Adopt a problem-solving approach to community issues** Work with the community partners and other agencies to solve community problems in accordance with the relevant legislation, policy, procedures and partnership agreements.
	112	**Conduct patrol** Conduct patrol responding to calls and requests for assistance, countering criminal activity and public disorder and minimising risks to public safety.
	123	**Prepare and drive police vehicles safely (operational)** Drive a police vehicle safely with consideration for others in accordance with organisational policy and in line with the system of car control.
	1031	**Remove vehicles** Remove vehicles safely and as authorised, in accordance with legislation and organisational policy.
	115	**Respond to road-related incidents, hazards, offences and collisions** Contribute to maintaining road safety by identifying and responding to hazards, regulating traffic, dealing with traffic offences and attending collision scenes in accordance with legislation and organisational policy.
Intelligence	57	**Use intelligence to support policing objectives** Use intelligence to support the achievement of community safety and crime reduction objectives. Ensure that intelligence is used ethically and in accordance with the relevant legislation, policy protocols and codes of practice.
Police Operations	69	**Prepare for and participate in planned policing operations** Participate in police and agency-led operations, working within appropriate authority limits and carrying out tasks necessary for the successful implementation of the operation while managing risks to the operation and acting in accordance with legislation and procedure.
	101	**Provide an initial response to incidents** Respond promptly and take control of the incident by correctly identifying the nature of the incident and take appropriate action to ensure that it is dealt with and recorded correctly.

Investigation	1	**Conduct initial investigation** Conduct the initial investigation and scene preservation in accordance with the relevant investigation policies and legal requirements, demonstrating support for victims and witnesses and recognising any possible impact on the community.
	33	**Manage scene preservation** Take charge of the scene taking appropriate action to ensure the initial preservation of the scene is complete, evaluate evidence, identify and pursue possible lines of enquiry as required to progress the investigation.
	74	**Provide care for victims and witnesses** Ensure that the necessary care for victims and witnesses is provided in an ethical and empathic manner and in accordance with the legislation, policies and procedures.
	52	**Search persons or personal property** Search individuals or personal property in accordance with the relevant legislation, policy and procedures, while respecting the dignity of the individual and being aware of the possible impact on the community.
Custody and Prosecution	42	**Prepare and present case files** Identify and present case materials, working with the Crown Prosecution Service or other relevant agencies/organisations to progress the case.
	44	**Present evidence in court and at other hearings** Attend court and give evidence in accordance with legislation.
Personal Responsibility	216	**Complete administration procedures** Ensure that all matters relating to the process of information are carried out in a prompt, efficient manner and in accordance with legislation, policy and procedure.
	206	**Comply with health and safety legislation** Ensure that you show a duty of care and take appropriate action to comply with health and safety requirements at all times.
	217	**Maintain standards of professional practice** Ensure your behaviour complies with organisational values and organise your own work effectively to meet the demands of your role. Identify, implement and monitor development activities to enhance your own performance.
	242	**Make best use of technology** Make best use of technology in support of your role, ensuring correct operation and compliance with organisational and legal requirements.
	141	**Promote equality, diversity and human rights in working practices** Promote equality, diversity and human rights in working practices by developing and maintaining positive working relationships, ensuring that colleagues are treated fairly and contributing to developing equality of opportunity in working practices.

	127	**Provide an organisational response recognising the needs of all communities** Build and maintain community relations by providing a service that is responsive to the needs of all communities and by ensuring that those affected by crime receive a fair and anti-discriminatory service.
Personal Responsibility	224	**Work as part of a team** Work co-operatively with team members and colleagues, contributing positively and constructively to the achievement of team and organisational objectives.
Managing the Organisation	236	**Participate in meetings** Prepare for and actively contribute within meetings in a clear, concise and relevant manner, ensuring decisions and actions are communicated to the appropriate personnel.
Health and Safety	207	**Provide first aid** Identify the nature of illness or injury and provide the necessary first aid treatment in accordance with approved procedures.

Behaviour Area	Level	Behaviour description
Working with Others	A	**Respect for race and diversity** Considers and shows respect for the opinions, circumstances and feelings of colleagues and members of the public, no matter what their race, religion, position, background, circumstances, status or appearance. Shows understanding for other people's views and takes them into account. Is tactful and diplomatic when dealing with people, treating them with dignity and respect at all times. Understands and is sensitive to social, cultural and racial differences.
	C	**Team working** Develops strong working relationships inside and outside the team to achieve common goals. Breaks down barriers between groups and involves others in discussions and decisions. Shows that they can work effectively as a team member and helps build relationships within it. Actively helps and supports others to achieve team goals.
	C	**Community and customer focus** Focuses on the customer and provides a high quality service that is tailored to meet their individual needs. Understands the communities that are served and shows an active commitment to policing that reflects their needs and concerns. Shows they can provide a high level of service to customers. Maintains contact with customers, works out what they need and responds to them.

		Effective communication Communicates ideas and information effectively, both verbally and in writing. Uses language and a style of communication that is appropriate to the situation and people being addressed. Makes sure that others understand what is going on.
	C	Shows they can speak clearly and concisely, and do not use jargon. Uses plain English and correct grammar. Listens carefully to understand.
Achieving Results		**Personal responsibility** Takes personal responsibility for making things happen and achieving results. Displays motivation, commitment, perseverance and conscientiousness. Acts with a high degree of integrity.
	B	Shows they can take personal responsibility for own actions and for sorting out issues or problems that arise. Is focused on achieving results to required standards and developing skills and knowledge.
		Resilience Shows resilience even in difficult circumstances. Prepared to make difficult decisions and has the confidence to see them through.
	B	Shows they have confidence to perform own role without unnecessary support in normal circumstances. Acts in appropriate way and controls emotions.

Appendix C

Witness statement: property

Form MG 11

WITNESS STATEMENT
(CJ Act 1967, s.9 MC Act 1980, ss.5A(3)(a) and 5B; MC Rules 1981, r.70)

Statement of: Ian MADSEN

Age if under 18:   O18   (if over 18 insert 'over 18')   Occupation: PCSO 5745

This statement (consisting of ...2... page(s) each signed by me) is true to the best of my knowledge and belief and I make it knowing that, if it is tendered in evidence, I shall be liable to prosecution if I have wilfully stated anything in it, which I know to be false, or do not believe to be true.

Signature: ....Ian Madsen..........PCSO 5745 ....   Date: 15th October 2006

Tick if witness evidence is visually recorded ☐ (supply witness details on rear)

At 1000hrs on Tuesday the 5th of September 2006 I was on duty in uniform carrying out foot patrol in the KINGSTON PARK estate when the local postman for the area, who I now know to be Dennis LEWIS, approached me. He stated that he had found some property that he believed to be suspicious at the rear of the KINGSTON PARK Community Centre and that he had not touched it but left it in situ. --------------------
----

I asked him to show me where he had found it. We arrived at the rear of the community centre, near to a store cabin that was situated five feet to the left of the rear entance of the community centre. Situated on the grassed area next to the store cabin door was the property that he identified to me. 1. Pair of black woollen gloves. 2. A small black torch 3. A yellow and blue flat screwdriver. He stated this was the property he had seen at around 7am that morning and that it did not appear to have moved since then. -------------------
----

I made a further search of the area around the community centre. Next to the compost bin a couple of feet away from where the gloves, torch and screwdriver were found I discovered a white plastic carrier bag containing a garden fork and trowel both with yellow handles, a pair of heavy duty gardening gloves and a roll of green gardening string. All of the items in the carrier bag looked old and well used and were still covered in dried mud. ---

I seized all of the items and transported them back to KINGSTON PARK police office where I placed each item in a separate bag and recorded the details on property form KP/191/06 as follows: -----------------------------
----

Signature: Ian Madsen...........PCSO 5745.......   Signature witnessed by: ....

2004/05(1): MG11

Continuation of Statement of Ian MADSEN..

1. Black woollen gloves — — — — — (IM1) --

2. Small black torch — — — — — — (IM2) --

3. Yellow and blue flat headed screwdriver — (IM3) --

4. Yellow handled garden fork — — — (IM4) --

5. Yellow handled trowel — — — — (IM5) --

6. Heavy duty garden gloves — — — (IM6) --

7. Green garden string — — — — — (IM7) --

8. White plastic carrier bag — — — — (IM8) --

I sealed each individual bag and labelled them accordingly with the property reference KP/191/06 and the corresponding exhibit number. --

These are my original exhibits and can be produced as evidence if required. I handed all eight sealed bags to the property clerk who placed them in the secure property store at Kingston Park police office. *Ian Madsen PCSO 5745*...

Signature: *Ian Madsen...........PCSO 5745.......*   **Signature witnessed by:** ....
2004/05(1): MG11(C)

RESTRICTED – FOR POLICE AND PROSECUTION ONLY
(when complete)

MG11

Home address: KINGSTON PARK POLICE OFFICE,
RED LANE, KINGSTON   Postcode: K22 R45

Home telephone No: N/A   Work telephone No: 0987654321

Mobile/Pager No: N/A   E-mail address: ian.madsen@kingston.police.uk

Preferred means of contact: ....

Male / ~~Female~~ (delete as applicable)   Date and place of birth: 14/09/1973 – Kingston

Former name: N/A   Height: 6' 2 "   Ethnicity Code: WI

Dates of witness non-availability: March 2007 and August 13th–31st 2007

Witness care

a) Is the witness willing and likely to attend court? Yes/No. If 'No', include reason(s) on MG6.
What can be done to ensure attendance?..

....

b) Does the witness require 'special measures' as a vulnerable or intimidated witness? Yes/No, If
'Yes' submit MG2 with file. ....

....

c) Does the witness have any specific care needs? Yes/No. If 'Yes' what are they? (healthcare, childcare,
transport, disability, language difficulties, visually imparied, restricted mobility or other concerns?)...

....

....

Witness Consent (for witness completion)

a) The criminal justice process and Victim Personal Statement scheme
(victims only) has been explained to me: Yes ☐ No ☐

b) I have been given the leaflet 'Giving a witness statement to police –
what happens next?':   Yes ☐ No ☐

c) I consent to police having access to my medical records in relation
to this matter: Yes ☐ No ☐ N/A ☐

d) I consent to my medical record in relation to this matter being
disclosed to the defence: Yes ☐ No ☐ N/A ☐

e) I consent to the statement being disclosed for the purposes of civil
proceedings e.g. child care proceedings (if applicable):   Yes ☐ No ☐ N/A ☐

f) The information recorded above will be disclosed to the Witness Service
so they can offer help and support, unless you ask them not to. Tick this   ☐
box to decline their services

Signature of witness: ....

Statement taken by (print name): ....

Station: ....

Time and place statement taken: ....

Signature of witness:...

2004/05(1): MG11

133

Appendix D

Witness statement: youth nuisance

Form MG 11

WITNESS STATEMENT
(CJ Act 1967, s.9 MC Act 1980, ss.5A(3)(a) and 5B; MC Rules 1981, r.70)

Statement of: Ian MADSEN

Age if under 18:   O18   (if over 18 insert 'over 18')   Occupation: PCSO 5745

This statement (consisting of ...2... page(s) each signed by me) is true to the best of my knowledge and belief and I make it knowing that, if it is tendered in evidence, I shall be liable to prosecution if I have wilfully stated anything in it, which I know to be false, or do not believe to be true.

Signature: ....*Ian Madsen*..........PCSO 5745 ....   Date: 15th October 2006

Tick if witness evidence is visually recorded ☐ (supply witness details on rear)

At approximately 2000hrs on Saturday 10th July 2006, I was on duty in uniform carrying out foot patrol in the area of the FERN GRANGE housing estate. ---

At this time I received information on my personal radio of a reported incident of youths causing a nuisance at the park situated at the rear of the shops on the High Street. ---

I entered the park from the High Street on the public footpath. The street lights were on and it was well lit. I could see two youths at the far end of the park approximately 30 feet away from my location. They appeared to be standing on one of the park benches jumping up and down and shouting loudly to the other youths that were standing around them. I started to walk towards them and these two youths remained on the park bench, they continued shouting out to each other and becoming abusive. --
----

When I got a couple of feet away I saw a youth I now know to be Jason WILKS (17yrs) who was one of the youths standing on the park bench, throw down a can of Coke onto the floor. I asked WILKS to pick up the can of Coke and place it in a litter bin at the shop opposite, he replied "NO". I again requested WILKS to pick up the can of Coke as he was commiting the offence of littering and could be liable for a fine or summons to court. He laughed and replied "NO CHANCE". --------------------I obtained and verified full details of WILKS and issued him a Littering fixed penalty ticket, which he accepted. WILKS was warned that if he did not comply with the instructions on the ticket that he may be liable for summons, I asked if WILKS understood this and he replied "YES I DO". ---

Signature: *Ian Madsen*...........PCSO 5745.......   Signature witnessed by: ....

2004/05(1): MG11

As I issued the ticket to WILKS I saw the other male who was standing on the park bench scrumple up a packet of crisps he was eating and throw it on the floor at the can that had been dropped previously. He turned to me and said, "HE MIGHT BE A WIMP, BUT I DON'T GIVE A FUCK WHAT YOU LOT SAY, WHAT ARE YOU GONNA DO NOW HOBBY BOBBY". He said this in an aggressive manner towards me, due to this, his size and also the numbers of other youths present at the scene I felt that my personal safety was under threat. I immediately took a step back away from the group of youths and requested that a police officer attend the park. I approached the youth that was standing up on the bench shouting the obscenities and outlined the offence of littering to him explaining that he could be fined or summonsed to court if he did not pick the litter up. He replied "FUCK OFF YOU ARE NOT EVEN A PROPER COP". I requested his name and address to which he replied "MICKEY MOUSE, I LIVE IN A HOUSE WITH MINNIE".

At this point a marked police vehicle pulled up and PC 1157 PERRIT and PC 457 FREEMAN spoke with me. I explained what had gone on and identified the youth to them that had thrown down the crisp packet and who had also been abusive towards me. I explained the full circumstances to PC PERRIT and FREEMAN. They approached the youth and he refused to give them his details and also refused to pick up the litter saying 'I DIDN'T DROP IT, I FUCKING DIDN'T SAY THAT, WHAT A FUCKING WANKER'. I saw PC PERRIT arrest the youth and place him in the police vehicle and he was transported away from the scene. I would describe the youth as follows – male, white, aged approximately 16-19years old, he was about 6'0' tall of medium build, he had short fair hair, which was gelled at the front into a small spike, he had a spotty complexion with lots of marks around his chin and nose. At the time of the incident he was wearing a blue and white hooped hooded top which was long sleeved and dark blue tracksuit bottoms. I cannot recall what he was wearing on his feet. I was only a couple of feet away from the youth at the shortest point during the incident and I had a clear unobstructed view of him. Although it was evening time there was a street light that was illuminated directly above the park bench where the youth was standing which lit the whole area giving good visibility. I had never seen the male youth before. The whole incident lasted for approximately 10 minutes from start to finish and during that time there were members of the public using the footpath through the park to the shops who witnessed this youth's behaviour and who could have overheard the foul language that he was using. *Ian Madsen PCSO 5274*

....
....
....
....
....
....
....
....
....
....
....
....
....
....
....
....
....

Signature: *Ian Madsen*...........PCSO 5745.......   Signature witnessed by: ....

2004/05(1): MG11(C)

RESTRICTED – FOR POLICE AND PROSECUTION ONLY
(when complete)

MG11

Home address: ....

.... Postcode: ....

Home telephone No: .... Work telephone No: ....

Mobile/Pager No: .... E-mail address: ....

Preferred means of contact: ....

Male / Female (delete as applicable)   Date and place of birth: ....

Former name: ....   Height: ....   Ethnicity Code: ....

Dates of witness non-availability: ....

....

Witness care

a) Is the witness willing and likely to attend court? Yes/No. If 'No', include reason(s) on MG6. What can be done to ensure attendance?...

....

b) Does the witness require 'special measures' as a vulnerable or intimidated witness? Yes/No. If 'Yes' submit MG2 with file ....

c) Does the witness have any specific care needs? Yes/No. If 'Yes' what are they? (healthcare, childcare, transport, disability, language difficulties, visually imparied, restricted mobility or other concerns?)...

....

....

Witness Consent (for witness completion)

a) The criminal justice process and Victim Personal Statement scheme (victims only) has been explained to me: Yes ☐ No ☐

b) I have been given the leaflet 'Giving a witness statement to police – what happens next?':   Yes ☐ No ☐

c) I consent to police having access to my medical records in relation to this matter: Yes ☐ No ☐ N/A ☐

d) I consent to my medical record in relation to this matter being disclosed to the defence: Yes ☐ No ☐ N/A ☐

e) I consent to the statement being disclosed for the purposes of civil proceedings e.g. child care proceedings (if applicable):   Yes ☐ No ☐ N/A ☐

f) The information recorded above will be disclosed to the Witness Service so they can offer help and support, unless you ask them not to. Tick this box to decline their services   ☐

Signature of witness: ....

Statement taken by (print name): ....

Station: ....

Time and place statement taken: ....

Signature of witness:..

2004/05(1): MG11

Appendix E

Witness statement: alcohol

Form MG 11

WITNESS STATEMENT
(CJ Act 1967, s.9 MC Act 1980, ss.5A(3)(a) and 5B; MC Rules 1981, r.70)

Statement of: Ian MADSEN

Age if under 18: O18 (if over 18 insert 'over 18') Occupation: PCSO 5745

This statement (consisting of ...2... page(s) each signed by me) is true to the best of my knowledge and belief and I make it knowing that, if it is tendered in evidence, I shall be liable to prosecution if I have wilfully stated anything in it, which I know to be false, or do not believe to be true.

Signature: ....Ian Madsen..........PCSO 5745 .... Date: 16th October 2006

Tick if witness evidence is visually recorded ☐ (supply witness details on rear)

At 1930hrs on Friday the 7th October 2006, I was on duty in uniform in company with PCSO 5721 FAWN, conducting foot patrol in the area of FERN GRANGE housing estate. At this time we entered the park area of FERN GRANGE when I saw approximately six youths sitting on a bench in the park. We approached them and as we got closer to the youths I saw that two of the youths stood up and placed an object behind their backs and stood closer together. I spoke to the youths on the bench and I noticed that there were a couple of empty Fosters Lager cans lying around the bench. I approached the two youths standing up who I now know to be Dean CORNWALL (16yrs) and Harvey FULLER (17yrs) and asked them what they had behind their backs. They handed to me a 1 litre bottle of White Lightning cider which was half full. While I was talking to CORNWALL and FULLER, PCSO FAWN had discovered a white carrier bag containing 8 cans of Fosters Lager; the cans were unopened and hidden under the nearby slide. ---
----

PCSO FAWN asked the youths whom the cans belonged to and they replied that they did not know. I requested Cornwall's and Fuller's full details and requested that they surrender the bottle of White Lightening cider. They both agreed to give up the cider, which I seized, and provided me with full details which I recorded on a PACE 1 form. At this point I obtained the names and addresses of all the youths present and then conducted checks to verify the details given. All of the youths were under 18yrs of age. --------------------
----

Signature: *Ian Madsen...........PCSO 5745.......* Signature witnessed by: ....

2004/05(1): MG11

PCSO FAWN also seized the 8 cans of Fosters Lager, as we believed that the youths did intend to drink them and that all the youths present were under 18. PCSO FAWN recorded all the details of the other youths present and informed them that the alcohol would be disposed of in an appropriate manner. Whilst talking to CORNWALL and FULLER I could smell intoxicating liquor on their breaths and I noticed that their eyes were glazed and their speech slightly slurred. I believed that they had been drinking and were drunk. As they were drunk and therefore vulnerable I requested transport to take them home so that they would be in the care of a responsible adult. A short time later a police vehicle arrived and transported them to their home address.

On our return to Kingston Park police office I conferred with Sergeant 1234 TOWNSEND and at 2015hrs I disposed of the White Lightening cider and eight cans of Fosters Lager in her presence, by pouring the contents into an outside drain. Before disposing of the containers I made a record of the bar codes for the bottle of cider and the cans of lager in my pocket notebook as follows: White Lightening Cider (1 litre bottle) bar code – 019873334211768, Eight cans of Fosters bar code – 004213777776900. Ian Madsen PCSO 5745

Signature: *Ian Madsen*...........PCSO 5745.......   Signature witnessed by: ....

2004/05(1): MG11(C)

RESTRICTED – FOR POLICE AND PROSECUTION ONLY
(when complete)

MG11

Home address: ....

.... Postcode: ....

Home telephone No: .... Work telephone No: ....

Mobile/Pager No: .... E-mail address: ....

Preferred means of contact: ....

Male / Female (delete as applicable)   Date and place of birth: ....

Former name: .... Height: .... Ethnicity Code: ....

Dates of witness non-availability: ....

....

Witness care

a) Is the witness willing and likely to attend court? Yes/No. If 'No', include reason(s) on MG6. What can be done to ensure attendance?...

....

b) Does the witness require 'special measures' as a vulnerable or intimidated witness? Yes/No. If 'Yes' submit MG2 with file ....

c) Does the witness have any specific care needs? Yes/No. If 'Yes' what are they? (healthcare, childcare, transport, disability, language difficulties, visually imparied, restricted mobility or other concerns?)...

....

....

Witness Consent (for witness completion)

a) The criminal justice process and Victim Personal Statement scheme (victims only) has been explained to me: Yes ☐ No ☐

b) I have been given the leaflet 'Giving a witness statement to police – what happens next?':   Yes ☐ No ☐

c) I consent to police having access to my medical records in relation to this matter: Yes ☐ No ☐ N/A ☐

d) I consent to my medical record in relation to this matter being disclosed to the defence: Yes ☐ No ☐ N/A ☐

e) I consent to the statement being disclosed for the purposes of civil proceedings e.g. child care proceedings (if applicable):   Yes ☐ No ☐ N/A ☐

f) The information recorded above will be disclosed to the Witness Service so they can offer help and support, unless you ask them not to. Tick this box to decline their services ☐

Signature of witness: ....

Statement taken by (print name): ....

Station: ....

Time and place statement taken: ....

Signature of witness:..

2004/05(1): MG11

Index